Writers Writing

Writers Writing

Lil Brannon
Melinda Knight
Vara Neverow-Turk

BOYNTON/COOK PUBLISHERS, INC.

Library of Congress Cataloging in Publication Data

Brannon, Lil.
  Writers writing.

  1. English language—Rhetoric.   I. Knight, Melinda.
II. Neverow-Turk, Vara.   III. Title.
PE1408.B667   1982   808'.042.   82-14587
  ISBN 0-86709-045-6

For information address Boynton/Cook Publishers, Inc.
206 Claremont Avenue, Montclair, NJ 07042

ISBN: 0-86709-043-X

Printed in the United States of America

82 83 84 85   10 9 8 7 6 5 4 3 2 1

Acknowledgments

(May 15, 1982)

This week the coffee maker bit the dust, just three days after the three-year full-service warranty ran out. So we estimate that it's time to abandon this text—no more drafts, no more rethinking, no more trying out chapters—not just because there's no coffee maker, but because after 2,387 cups of coffee, we now believe that it's time to abandon this text.

We certainly don't take this decision lightly. Every moment we have spent thinking and writing has also meant that others had to plan their lives and work around us—especially the NYU Expository Writing Program staff. The program lived with us through this enterprise—tried chapters out on students, read and reacted to portions of the book. And they never complained when there was no coffee on Monday. They just figured that we had worked during the weekend and would bring in a can the first time we got a chance.

It's been a long while since we collected the pieces in this book—work which we read as teachers, as friends, or as students. For all those who contributed, it's time to be finished.

Particularly thanks to friends and colleagues

Jocelyn Benford	Paula Johnson
Ann Berthoff	Cy Knoblauch
Bob Boynton	Pat Lisella
James Britton	Nancy Neil
Connie Doyle	Cindy Onore
David Echols	Gordon Pradl
Brian Egan	Carla Stern
Diane Ford	Joe Teper
Dixie Goswami	David Turk

And to students and colleagues whose work appears in this book with their permission:

Bill Atwill
David Bogoslaw
Bob Brown
Bill Burns
Paula Carmichael
Scott Edwards
Eric Hoffert
Sharyn Kassin
Kathryn Lance
Deborah Laniado
Lee Leeson
Bob Leonard

Sara Lewis
Maria Maggenti
Patrick McGrath
Stephanie Oppenheim
John Polizzotto
Dianne Ray
Blas Royo
Brian Santo
Rico Simonini
Nancy Sommers
Timothy Tseng

And purrticularly thanks to Sandra Boynton for her portraits of Writers Writing.

Contents

I want to ask you to be my inspiration,
to infatuate my humble senses with
your pure and unearthly fire, to startle
my slumbering consciousness with a
vivid rapture beyond all imagining.

Boynton ©

But I just can't seem to find the right words.

Writers Writing

Introduction
(Not the Usual Hogwash)

This book is not the usual hogwash about writing. You won't find grammar drills or handbook exercises; you won't find a chapter on the paragraph or lessons on description, narration, exposition, and argument. This book is not just another collection of rules and model essays. Your teacher will not lecture from it and probably won't assign it chapter by chapter. It won't provide you with skills to be mastered, or introduce you to progressively harder concepts to be learned and applied.

In fact, this book is not a textbook at all; rather, it's what Ken Macrorie calls a "context book,"[1] a book which demands that your own writing be the real focus of concern, so that you learn to write by writing and learn to reformulate by internalizing the questions of readers. The context is a writing workshop, a place where you write, read what you've written, and revise your initial drafts in response to readers' questions. The book dramatizes this process by showing not only what composing looks like but also what it feels like, providing you with glimpses of how other writers, experienced and inexperienced, have used their own powers of perception and the responses of readers to see their writing in new ways. You'll not only hear professional and student writers talk about their composing processes, but you'll also watch them as they write, seeing their tentative early drafts and the choices they made to develop their ideas into finished pieces of writing. You'll see writers test options and change their minds, watch them go in one direction and then abandon it for another, watch them decide that more explicit description is needed here or that an entire section should be cut out there.

The writing strategies dramatized in this book are those of real writers attempting to make meaning of their experiences, to learn more and more about a subject, beginning with a germ of an idea and exploring every way it could possibly grow. Their decisions, the strategies they have chosen, provide you with an orientation to the crucial

1

features of composing: discovering intentions, using writing to learn, thinking about readers, and talking to other writers about what to write and about what has been written. The book doesn't insist on these activities abstractly; it demonstrates their importance by showing you many different writers engaged in them. You won't be exposed to rules and formulas; rather, you will be given a way of viewing writing: that it is fluid and spontaneous, that it is not a fixed sequence of activities (first you make the outline . . .), that what writers say is guided by the effects they are trying to create, that writing-and-revising is one act—forming, thinking, and writing[2] happen all at once.

A writer does not go through a stage of preparing to write, and then a stage of writing neat and complete successive drafts, and then a stage of revising, polishing, and editing. Instead, writing and revising are synonymous. Revising begins before you even set pen to paper, while you're still sorting and selecting ideas. You may revise your first sentence repeatedly before you ever put a word on the page. And the process of writing-and-revising goes on even after you have typed the last period. No piece of writing is ever absolutely finished—there are always flaws, loose ends, and rough spots—but there are also deadlines. Rather than being like the novelist in Albert Camus's *The Plague,* who revised his first sentence perpetually but never wrote the rest of the story, you must be willing to leave a piece imperfect while at the same time trying to make it as good as it can be.

Writing-and-revising, like composing music or any other creative act, is the struggle to organize the chaos of experience. The composer John Cage once said that "what we call silence is only sounds that are not intended," and this "silence" is the chaos that a writer's intentions organize and make meaningful. Robert Pirsig observes in *Zen and the Art of Motorcycle Maintenance* that "the nature of the material at hand determines [your] thoughts and motions, which simultaneously change the nature of the material at hand. The material and your thoughts are changing together in a progression of changes until your mind's at rest at the same time the material is right." The process of writing is this progression of changes, and that's why fill-in-the-blanks, paint-by-the-numbers writing formulas do not work. Writing is a creative act, not an assembly-line operation of locking words together into sentences and bolting sentences together into paragraphs in accordance with a predefined plan.

This book will help you develop your writing abilities by asking you to write often and for different purposes. You'll be working on your own writing, on papers assigned for this class as well as papers assigned in other classes you're taking. At the end of each chapter, a series of *Writing-and-Revising* assignments will suggest ways of using such resources as personal experience, interviews, and library research as the basis for extended pieces of writing. In most chapters, there's at least one Writing-and-Revising option that goes beyond the boundaries of your writing class, involving you in writing for other classes and about other disciplines you're interested in. In addition, you'll be asked to keep a journal of your perceptions and experiences as a way of gathering material for your writing. You'll also use your journal to record how different pieces of writing you're working on develop, thus keeping track of your progress as a writer. You should write in your journal often (perhaps even every day), thinking of it as a place to experiment.

Further, you'll interact with what other writers have written. In most of the *Interactions,* you should "think with your pencil"; in other words, you should be constantly using writing as a way of seeing what you mean, writing down in the margins of the book your perceptions of what other writers are saying and speculating about the changes they make in their texts.

Your response to any writing assignment should be solidly grounded in what you already know, in what genuinely interests you, and in what you really want to know more about. Once you've established a starting point, you can discover what research you'll need to do to supplement and enrich your own ideas. You can gather research material from primary sources (interviews, original art works, poems, stories, letters, historical documents, scientific experiments) and from secondary sources—the work of other researchers (art critics, historians). You can track down some of your primary sources and most of your secondary sources by using abstracts, indexes, bibliographies, and reference works. Strong writing emerges from the confidence of being familiar with the territory, but it's only through the process of writing that familiarity becomes possible—the writing itself is a form of exploration, indeed, a form of research.

Your writing workshop will help you develop your abilities as a writer by asking you to interact with readers. Receiving responses to your work helps you determine what you have said and what still needs to be said. Although you are ultimately responsible for the ideas in your writing, readers can help you see how well your ideas are coming across. But remember, your readers can't give you easy answers or formulas that will automatically make your piece better. Your writing will improve only through experimentation, through writing something one way and then trying it another, through writing something down and trying it out on readers. You must feel free to take risks, seeing that having said something one way doesn't rule out saying it another way. You need the chance to try out new ways of presenting your ideas, discovering how many different ways you can view the same experience, trusting in your ability to continually re-envision your thoughts. This experimentation can be done only in a context where you can try out the options available to you without penalty.

Ultimately, you must determine what you want to say and what effect saying-it-this-way will have. Just as you learned to speak by trial and error in a supportive context, so you will gain competence and confidence in writing by similar experimentation. You'll learn to trust that readers are interested in what you're saying and will respond to the ideas you're presenting, that they'll tell you what they've heard and describe its effect on them, if you're willing to ask. One way your teacher will provide a supportive environment for writing is to ask you to submit working drafts for peer review and for teacher commentary, procedures that will be explained in the book. For this approach to work well, you must be aware of some of the basic assumptions that underlie it. First of all, you are the sole "owner" of your writing. You're responsible for the ideas presented and the choices made in creating your text. Second, you write in order to learn about a subject, and what you write communicates what you've discovered. These assumptions bring with them an important responsibility for you as a member of a writing workshop. You have a responsibility as a reader to tell others when their writing has confused you and to describe how the writing has surprised you, pleased you, or disappointed your expectations. Your teacher, an experienced reader, will model the reading and responding process for you. The result of careful, sensitive reading and responding is dialogue and negotiation. Writers know best what they want to say; readers know best what has been communicated and what effects have been created. A reader can't tell a writer what to do next, nor can a writer tell readers how they should have felt. The process of negotiation is a part of the process of re-envisioning a draft. The writer asks a reader "What would happen if I said it this way?" or "How is that different from saying it like this?"

You'll also learn to become your own reader, to heighten your sensitivity to and awareness of your own language. Every writer repeatedly rereads what he or she has written and this doubling back in order to be able to move forward is fundamental to the nature of writing. Like a painter who creates an irregular area of pale blue-green or highlights a pear and then stands back to get a sense of the entire composition in order to determine what to do next, you must "stand back" and look at what you've done before you can make new choices. Part of that reflection on what you've written, part of getting perspective on your work, is being objective enough to admire and appreciate rather than simply to judge. The richness of writing is in the pleasure of realizing that you have created something that you *like*.

The material found in the book is not a substitute for the interactive context of a writing workshop. Though the book will not prescribe how interaction is to happen, it does assume that it will happen. It will also show it happening, providing instances of writers changing their texts as a result of interacting with readers. The material in the book is analogous to the material you and your classmates will produce in the workshop, but it cannot substitute for it. This book is a resource, a common context, that the writers and readers in the workshop can share. But everyone must take the next step by learning to interact, to share the writing/reading experience with each other.

The book also creates an attitude about composing, showing that all writers begin somewhere in the chaos of their preliminary ideas and write their way into meaning. Many inexperienced writers believe that good writers never have trouble writing—that good writing springs fully edited from the pen. By providing you with drafts in progress to examine, this book demonstrates that seldom, if ever, is this assumption valid. Writers change their minds and redraft; they experiment with different ways of saying something; they need response from experienced readers, seek it out, and rewrite to meet the readers' needs. Accordingly, you'll have the chance to do these things in your workshop.

However, you won't be told explicitly how to change a piece of writing in order to make it better. No one can do that, although many books and teachers have tried. Other books use finished pieces of writing as models for you to emulate. They tell you what characterizes good writing by analyzing the features of a professional writer's text. But that is much like asking you to paint like Picasso by describing for you the features of *Guernica*. What describing the painting doesn't do is tell you how Picasso began working on it, using photographs and news releases from the bombed Basque town to make at least fifty studies before the painting itself began to take shape. The final canvas doesn't show how Picasso was constantly rearranging the composition before he was satisfied with the placement of the figures. What seeing a painting in a museum doesn't do is tell you how the artist composed: how many preliminary sketches he drew, how he mixed the paint, how he reshaped his ideas—all the false starts, all the dead-ends, all the choices, all the decisions that preceded the final product.

Writing is like painting—a creative process of continually making choices. This book will show you what happens before a piece of writing is finished, those choices the writers made—the selecting, ordering, questioning, and changing, the trying again. Writers achieve form by discovering what they want to say. They do not begin with a set of specifications, a blueprint, or an ideal form. Structure and organization are consequences of a search for meaning, not something you start out with. In other words, you create an order and then rely on your reader to recognize the connections you have made among ideas.

If that order is not apparent, if the writing appears illogical or disjointed, if you haven't made all the connections so that the line of reasoning can be followed, your reader can help by indicating what is confusing. Your reader can't, however, tell you the ideal way to "fix" a piece of writing. If someone does tell you how to fix what you've written, he or she can only be describing how he or she would have written it, not how you ought to change it. And in effect, you would no longer be in control of the writing—you would be taking dictation.

In the last chapter of the book, we talk about how we wrote *Writers Writing,* how we got the idea, and how we got through the obstacle course of making that idea into a book. The idea changed, grew, and developed as we put it into words, crossed out words, wrote new words, and got new ideas which then demanded more words. But that's what writers writing do and that's what writing-and-revising is all about. The final section of the book, "Suggestions for Teachers (Not for Teachers Only)," explains in greater theoretical depth the concepts introduced here and also includes practical suggestions for using the book as well as statements from four teachers describing how they used the book in their classrooms.

This book is an invitation to look over the shoulders of writers as they write, seeing that the way they go about it—whether they are students or professionals—is not too different from the way you do. Their tentative beginnings are not radically different from your own. Their uncertainties, confusions, and questions are part of the writing process itself. By having the opportunity to watch these writers compose, you'll see how their writing process works for them, how they shape fragmentary insights slowly into finished prose. By exploring in detail how other writers write, you'll be better able to understand and control your own writing strategies. You can also learn what new strategies are available to strengthen your writing. Finally, you may be able to change writing habits that do not help you. In other words, the composing activities of the writers in this book can become your landmarks and maps for charting your course as a writer.

Notes

1. Ken Macrorie used the term "context book" in an essay published on September 3, 1979 (A15) in *The New York Times.*
2. The terms forming/thinking/writing are the title of a textbook by Ann E. Berthoff (Montclair, N.J.: Boynton/Cook, 1979). Her strategies for writing-and-revising are helpful to anyone interested in developing control over their writing process.

Chapter 1

The Way You Write

I sit at my new desk. I get up and bolt my door open (a welcome sign to visitors). Okay. The phone is within reach. Okay. I have a light to work by. Okay. Pens? Check (pens ($\checkmark$)). I get out my notebook, open it, poise a pen over the first line, then begin to search for an idea. My vision rests on the bottom poster above my desk: TO SOLVE PROBLEMS—CLOSE YOUR EYES UNTIL THEY GO AWAY. I close my eyes and open them moments later; the assignment sheet is still there and the notebook page is still blank, I am amusing no one. I look at the top poster: WHENEVER I FEEL LIKE STUDYING I LIE DOWN UNTIL THE FEELING GOES AWAY. Definitely an attitude conducive to my wanting to write. . . .

BRIAN ROBERT SANTO

When the deadline would not go away, Brian became a writer. He did what he had to do in order to fill the blank pages with whatever he found to say. He wrote and rewrote, scribbled and crossed out, began and then began again. Although you may have been told that the best way to write is to construct an outline and begin each paragraph with a topic sentence, Brian's writing process—the way he goes about writing—is quite different. Yet Brian is a good writer.

What does he do that makes him a good writer? Like all writers, he is constantly looking at himself as a writer in order to discover writing strategies that work. No matter what your level of ability or your effectiveness as a writer, knowing what works for you and what gets in the way of your doing your best work is the first step in improving your own ability to write. In this chapter, you begin the process of exploring yourself as a writer and of discovering what really works for you.

Writing Profile

We have put together a set of questions that will enable you to construct your profile as a writer. There are no wrong answers; the right ones are simply your perceptions of yourself as a writer. You may be tempted to answer just yes or no to these questions, but it's important that you answer each one as fully as possible. Or you may want to leave out certain information that seems trivial to you, yet even the smallest detail is helpful in understanding the way you write.

Answer all of the following questions by writing down as much information as you can. By answering carefully, you'll discover what you do when you write.

□   □   □

Writing Profile Questionnaire

1. What sorts of writing do you do most often? Least often? Why? List all the kinds of writing you do. What kind do you enjoy most? When writing for class, would you rather have the teacher give you the subject or would you rather find one yourself? Why?
2. How do you feel about your writing?
3. What experiences have affected your learning how to write? Did someone show you or tell you how to write? If so, what were you told? Do you do what you were told? If no one ever taught you how to write, how did you learn?
4. What is the hardest part of writing for you? The easiest part?
5. How do you start a piece of writing? How do you find out what you want to say?
6. Where do you prefer to be when you're writing? (For example, do you have a favorite chair or a particular spot in the library? Do you write best at night or early in the morning?) What materials do you use when you write? (For example, do you prefer yellow legal pads and a ball point pen?)
7. Do you write more than one draft of a piece of writing? If so, why? If not, why not?
8. What does the concept of revising mean to you?
9. Are you willing to read your writing to other people? Who do you read it to? Do you ever read a piece of your writing to anyone before it's finished? Do you reread your writing? If so, what do you reread it for?
10. How do you know when a piece of writing is finished? Do you worry about not being able to finish a piece of writing?
11. What do you think the characteristics of "good" writing are? Is you writing "good" writing? Why or why not?

□   □   □

What follows is a series of what we're calling *Interactions*. We're asking you to interact not only with concepts in this book, but also with your classmates, your teachers, and other writers. Interactions provide ways to explore your own writing process by asking questions, by writing to discover what you mean, and by reading to see what you and other writers are saying. Interactions, of course, are only the beginning; it will be up to you to decide what writing-and-revising strategies work best for you.

Interactions

- Compare your writing profile with those of your classmates.
    What similarities do you see? What differences? To what do you attribute these similarities and differences?
- How do you think your writing profile would be similar to or different from those of less experienced writers? From more experienced writers?

□   □   □

The matter of revising gets little attention in most writing texts. It's central to this one. What follows are the answers of various writers to Question 8: "What does the concept of revising mean to you?"

Some high school students felt revising means:

"do it until you get it right"
"change parts of what I have written until I am satisfied with it"
"find mistakes in my paper"
"look for spelling and grammatical errors"
"look for overused words and take out dumb things"
"get rid of my mistakes"

College freshmen answered:

"I say scratch out and do over and that means what it says: scratching out and cutting out. I read what I have written and I cross out a word and put another word in—a more decent word or a better word. Then if there is somewhere to use a sentence that I have crossed out, I will put it there."

"I just review every word and make sure that everything is worded right. I see if I am rambling. I see if I can put a better word in or leave one out. Usually when I read what I have written, I say to myself, 'that word is so bland or so trite,' and then I go and get my thesaurus."

"Redoing means just using better words and eliminating words that are not needed. I go over and change words around."

"I don't use the word *revising* because I only write one draft and the changes that I make are made on top of that draft. The changes that I make are usually just marking out words and putting in different ones."

"I throw things out and say they are no good. I like to write like Fitzgerald did by inspiration and if I feel inspired then I don't need to slash and throw out much."

Some experienced professional writers understood revising to mean:

"It is a matter of looking at the kernel of what I have written, the content, and then thinking about it, responding to it, making decisions, and actually restructuring."

"I rewrite as I write. It is hard to tell what is a first draft because it is not determined by time. In one draft, I might cross out three pages, write two, cross out a fourth, rewrite it, and call it a draft. I am constantly writing and rewriting. I can only conceptualize so much in my first draft—only so much information can be held in my head at one time: my rewriting efforts are a reflection of how much information I can encompass at one time. There are levels and agenda which I have to attend to in each draft."

"Rewriting means on one level, finding the argument, and on another level language changes to make the argument more effective. Most of the time I feel as if I can go on rewriting forever. There is always one part of a piece that I could keep working on. It is always difficult to know at what point to abandon a piece of writing. I like this idea that a piece of writing is never finished, just abandoned."

"My first draft is usually very scattered. In rewriting, I find the line of the argument. After the argument is resolved, I am much more interested in word choice and phrasing."

"My cardinal rule in revising is never to fall in love with what I have written in a first or second draft. An idea, sentence, or even a phrase that looks catchy—I don't trust. Part of this idea is to wait awhile. I am much more in love with something after I have written it than I am a day or two later. It is much easier to change anything with time."

"Revising means taking apart what I have written and putting it back together again. I ask major theoretical questions of my ideas, respond to those questions, and think of proportion and structure. I try to find a controlling metaphor and in doing that I find out which ideas can be developed and which should be dropped. I am constantly chiseling and changing as I revise."

Nancy Sommers, "Revision Strategies of Student Writers and Experienced Adult Writers," *College Composition and Communication,* Vol. 31, No. 4, December, 1980, pp. 380–81, 383–4. Reprinted by permission.

Interactions

- What differences do you see between the responses of high school students and college freshmen? Between college freshmen and professional writers?
- Make a general statement about how each group sees revision.
- Compare your own answer to Question 8 with the responses of these writers. What are the differences and similarities? How do you account for these differences and similarities?

□   □   □

Writing-and-Revising One

(a) Write a paper in which you describe the writing profile of one of your classmates. Don't just use the writer's responses to the questionnaire; interview him or her to get some personal background. If possible, read some of this writer's previous work (an essay from high school, a letter, a poem, a journal entry).

Save all your notes and drafts—anything you write down and use. You'll want to look at these later as you further define your own writing-and-revising process.

(b) Show the profile to the writer. Ask if all the information is accurate and clear. Ask about what kinds of changes he or she would like to see in the profile. (For example, is there any other information that should be included?)

Now rewrite the profile.

Chapter 2

The Writing-and-Revising Process

> I don't have any idea *how* to get something right; I just
> know when it is. . . . the whole thing is a process of trial and
> error: writing, and then looking at it as a reader; making
> changes, then rereading again.
>
> KATHRYN LANCE

Kathryn Lance, a professional writer, is writing about her writing process. Writing to her—and to most writers, both student and professional—is a process of trial and error, of writing and reading, of rewriting and rereading. Interestingly, many people do not realize that writers write this way. They believe that good writers know exactly what they're going to say, that they don't have to go through the process of trial and error, that they don't have any difficulties in writing. They make the following assumptions about good writers:

1. Good writing results from a flash of inspiration.
2. Good writers know exactly what they want to say before they begin.
3. Good writers begin with an outline and expand it into sentences.
4. Good writers always have a thesis statement and begin each paragraph with a topic sentence.
5. Good writers have in their heads a set of models from which they choose a particular form.
6. Good writers know what their readers need to know.
7. Good writers never show their writing to anyone else until it's finished.
8. Good writers find writing easy.
9. Good writers don't procrastinate.
10. Good writers never have to revise.

How many of these assumptions have you heard before or do you yourself believe? If you share these assumptions, it may be because you've seen only the finished versions of a writer's work. Polished writing looks as if it were easy for the writer to do. Every word is in its right place and spelled correctly. Everything is ordered and logically developed. But what you don't know is how the writer got there. Seldom does anyone get a chance to talk to good writers and find out what they actually do. If you could, you would learn that these assumptions are false nearly all the time, as you can see from reading Lance's description of her writing process.

Interactions

- As you read Lance's essay, note in the margin each time she either conforms to or departs from any of the assumptions about good writers listed above.

□   □   □

HOW I WRITE

Kathryn Lance

I have been a full-time professional writer for over ten years. In that time I have written five nonfiction books, hundreds of television soap opera scripts, several articles for women's magazines, and many dozens of articles, stories, scripts, and teaching guides for Scholastic Magazines, where I was for a time on staff. I've published nationally only one piece of adult fiction, in 1969.

In all my writing I have always revised very heavily. I used to hope that as I got better I would have to revise less, but the opposite seems to be happening: as I gain more experience I become more self-critical and spend even more time on rewriting and polishing.

I've concluded that I--and any other writers who spend a great deal of time on revision--probably put down on paper much of what other writers do in their heads: which is to say nearly everything, including initial ideas, alternative word choices, sudden (often abortive) bright ideas for new directions, and of course all normal "polishing" procedures, such as cuts, word changes, and reorganization.

Examining my own revision process has turned out to be very difficult. I thought it would be easy to figure out why I did something at a given point, but often I can only guess. It's very easy to say, "Well, it sounds better that way," but quite another thing to state _why_ it sounds better. A lot of my writing and rewriting

seems to come from an area beneath or beyond my consciousness. I
have discovered, however, that there are a number of general principles I follow, which I've attempted to articulate here. Also
I've unconsciously devised several editorial markings which I
use consistently and can easily decipher. These are explained as
they occur.

The material I will examine is from Pandora's Genes, an as-
yet unpublished science fiction novel that I have written. All of
the novel underwent multiple, extensive revisions and polishes.
Not all drafts remain. However, just before the novel was submit-
ted to Ballantine Books, an editor friend suggested making two
changes at the end. These involved expanding one scene to include
some crucial new material, and adding another, short scene.

Of the two changes, by far the most difficult was the first.
At times I despaired of ever getting it right, and considered simply leaving the old scene as it was. Eventually, however, I got it
into satisfactory shape. In this paper I will try to examine how I
did that.

The scene is short and the total revision amounted to an ex-
pansion from nine to thirteen paragraphs. Of the total, nine paragraphs were new or revised. Nevertheless, I went through sixteen
separate stages of revision.

As a preliminary note, I'd like to discuss how I write and revise, and what I think goes on at each stage. The process for me is
always the same, whether I am writing fiction, nonfiction, or
scripts.

First, almost always, I begin with notes, which may in some
cases consist of extensive scribbles, and in other cases just a
word or two indicating what I need to do. For example, the preliminary notes for the present revisions were scribbled on a cocktail
napkin immediately after the conversation with the editor who had
suggested the changes. The notes were brief (I no longer have
them), and said something like, "Z-Princ. scene alone, succession."

I didn't need any further information. What the note meant to
me was that I had to have a scene between Zach and the Principal
alone (before the last scene), and that in that scene or an earlier
one they had to discuss the problem of the succession (the Principal is the unmarried, childless leader of an empire). My editor
friend had suggested that the succession could be covered in the
new scene, but I knew--without thinking about it--that the succession belonged in an earlier scene which I had never been completely happy with. As for the new scene, my friend felt it was
necessary dramatically for a number of reasons, and I again in-

stantly realized what had to happen in that scene. Indeed, it is so important to the denouement of the novel I can't understand why I didn't write it in the first place. (A friend who has just had a book published to critical acclaim said that the same thing happened with his novel, that several people told him he had to insert one scene just before the end of the book. Once he had done so, he saw that the scene was inevitable and necessary. He told me it brought back his mother's advice: "If three people tell you you're drunk, lie down.")

Where to put the new material solved my first problem, that of structure. To continue with the discussion of the process:

Once I know _what_ must be covered in a scene or chapter or section, and where it should go, I then write a first draft. Almost always I do so very quickly (as fast as I can type), with some reference to whatever notes I have before me, but usually not thinking about it very much at all. Sometimes I write this draft with only the vaguest idea of what will happen (or what will be explained, in nonfiction). The result is often just short of incoherent--full of typos, incomplete sentences, infelicities of language, much repetition, etc. In short, this first draft is what James Thurber referred to as "mud." Once it has been written, the first draft is put aside for at least a few hours, and usually for a day or more. (When I go back to this first draft I almost always find that it is better than I thought while writing it, and sometimes that it has some very good things in it, although it is usually incoherent and unreadable, except by me.)

The next step is to look the first draft over and make rough pencil changes and suggestions. I have discovered that I've devised unconsciously a series of editorial markers: for instance, a wavy line in the margin means that a section is not right as it stands; "exp" means to expand; a question mark means I'm not sure whether to keep this or not. When I see that something else is needed, I make notes to myself in the margin. At this reading of the first draft I may go over it several times, or only once. Unless it is now close to final form I usually set it aside again for a while.

After I have gone over the first draft (in one or several sittings) until it is completely marked up, I generally retype (revising as I do). The purpose of this is to clean up what I have so far, enabling me to see how much more work there is to do. I then go over this new material as I did with the first draft, marking it up in one or more sittings. I continue to go through this process: pencil-work, inserts, etc., followed by retyping and more pencil-work, inserts, and so on, until what I have is right. Depending on the given work it may be as few as two complete drafts (retypings) or as many as twenty or more.

At some point I achieve what I consider a type-ready script, and then either give it to a typist or type it myself. If I type it myself I usually make a few more minor changes as I go along.

Because of the extensive work I do, the terms "draft" and "polish" don't really apply to my revisions. I realize now that what I really do is go through different stages, each of which may include extensive rewriting as well as finer, "polish" work.

The above describes the mechanics of what I do. The mental processes are more complex, and I don't fully understand them. I am not in a normal mental state when I write, revise, or polish. The original writing sometimes seems outside my control, as if it were happening automatically (this is true for both fiction and non-fiction). However, it does not happen at all until I have become steeped in the subject and thought about it a great deal, both consciously and unconsciously. I almost always have a hard time getting myself to sit and begin writing (first drafting). I usually trick myself, saying that I'll just work for five or ten minutes. Usually, the material takes over and I stay for as long as it takes to complete the section I am writing.

When I revise I work much, much more slowly. I can spend an hour or more on one paragraph if necessary. And my concentration is close to total. I do not notice the passage of time, I do not notice what is going on around me, sometimes I don't even hear the phone. As I explained above, I do all this in stages (and very occasionally something is right the first time or by the second stage). I think of it all as a whittling down process, as if I were making something like a carved figurine or a clay pot with my hands. With each successive pass over the material I try to make it cleaner and better-structured and closer to what the final form will be. It is a process of selection: taking out things that don't belong and trying other things to see if they do. Often I struggle with a paragraph or whole section that I can't imagine how to fix; sometimes I manage to fix it, but I have learned that if something just doesn't seem fixable after many tries, it probably doesn't belong in any form and should simply be cut. If the thing that should be cut is something that I particularly like, I will often resist throwing it out until the whole rest of the passage is right and I see that the "little gem" absolutely has to go.

I don't have any idea how to get something right; I just know when it is. I have picked up some tricks of the trade over the years--for example, if a nonfiction piece is moving slowly, it's probably time to put in an anecdote--but mostly, for me, the whole thing is a process of trial and error. Writing, and then looking at it as a reader; making changes, then reading again. I have also found that if I <u>accept</u> the fact that I must rewrite a great deal and slowly, and don't worry about the time spent, I can eventually hammer anything into shape, no matter how hopeless it may appear at first.

Interactions

- As you read Lance's paper, what, if anything, surprised you? Compare your own profile as a writer with her description of her writing process. What differences and similarities do you see? To what do you attribute these differences and similarities?
- Make a list of those things which you as a writer have in common with her as a writer.
- On the basis of your notes on Lance's essay, construct a new list of assumptions about good writers.

□   □   □

Because Lance is a professional, she has become highly conscious about what she does as a writer. Brian Santo, a student writer, has also looked closely at his writing process. What do you notice about it that is similar to Lance's?

Interactions

- As you read Brian's essay, note in the margins any evidence that supports or contradicts your new assumptions about good writers.

□   □   □

THE <u>REASON</u> <u>GOD</u> <u>MADE</u> <u>HANDS</u>

Brian Robert Santo

Comfort/Convenience

I have no fixed pattern for writing until I discover the way of situating myself for maximum convenience and comfort. I simply have to be comfortable when I write. I have to have everything I need right there at hand before I feel ready to write. Specifically, what I have to do is go through a process of identifying my distractions and then cataloguing them as internal (comfort) or external (convenience), and then systematically finding the most desirable way of dealing with them. What that means is that I find the easiest way for each distraction to be as close to 100% effective as I can get it.

Going Through the Process Again: A New Home

Okay, so here I am at NYU. I have to write a paper for English. Okay, I'm in college, so I have to pretend I'm a college student. Here we go. Okay. I'm rolling now. College students have their own desks to work at. I look at my desk. It looks something like this:

. . . Not particularly appealing to me either, but, I tell myself, when in college, you have to do as the collegians do . . .

Attempt Number One

I sit at my new desk. I get up and bolt my door open (a welcome sign to visitors). Okay. The phone is within reach. Okay. I have a light to work. Okay. Pens? Check (pens (✓)). I get out my notebook, open it, poise a pen over the first line, then begin to search for an idea. My vision rests on the bottom poster above my desk: TO SOLVE PROBLEMS--CLOSE YOUR EYES UNTIL THEY GO AWAY. I close my eyes and open them moments later; the assignment sheet is still there and the notebook page is still blank. I am amusing no one. I look at the top poster: WHENEVER I FEEL LIKE STUDYING I LIE DOWN UNTIL THE FEELING GOES AWAY.

Definitely an attitude conducive to my wanting to write . . .

I am not optimistic about writing here. Writing at a desk generally comes with bad karma. The chair I'm in is uncomfortable. The desktop is too small. The view stinks. The desk is ugly (see diagram). Bluntly, I don't like it.

I force myself to write. The finished product turns out to rank among the worst efforts at writing I've ever made.

Attempt Number Two

My desk, I decide, is an inappropriate place to write because its function is to provide a place to write and therefore is totally ineffective for doing so. Also, it is not comfortable. Nor does it have any strategic value for convenience. Before I even had my second writing assignment, I knew I would not write it at my desk.

Whither, then, should I do my writing? The most comfortable place in the room is my bed, and I decide to try it out for writing. I bolt the door open (a welcome sign to visitors), slip a tape into my tape deck and press "play." I put the phone within reach. All set. I pull out my journal first. Things are running around in my head and writing provides a cathartic exercise in thought exorcism. This accomplished, I get out my notebook, and once again lie down on my tummy on my bed, which looks like this:

Hey, you know about bachelor pads . . .

Anyway, I find that lying on my tummy is not a comfortable way to write. Nor is writing on my side. Writing on my back is quickly proven to be impossible. By the end of the evening I was forced to admit to myself that even though I was, on the whole, satisfied with my paper, my bed is _not_ a comfortable place to write.

Attempt Number Three

I eye my bed suspiciously. I look at my desk ruefully. I am running out of places to write. In fact, there is only one place

left, and it looks questionable in terms of comfort and it has no
tactical value for convenience. It is a black vinyl monstrosity in
between my roommate's desk and my dresser. It looks something like
this:

. . . The furniture <u>never</u> matches in NYU dorms . . .

I sit in the chair and lo and behold! It's comfortable! I set-
tle my buns in and so pleased am I that I have found a place to
write, that I neglect my distractions. I write a pretty good paper.

Attempt Number Four

I now have a place to sit. There are preparations that need to
be made, for I have much to write this day. I need to make another
journal entry, do a paper for psych, and write an essay for English. First, I take my desk chair and position it across from my
comfy black monstrosity. I heap some foam rubber on the seat and I
have a place to prop my feet comfortably. I bolt the door open (a
welcome sign to visitors). I take my roommate's desk chair and
pull it next to the comfy chair; on the seat of this I put the tele-
phone. I place the phonebook next to me so I can distract myself by
calling my friends if they don't call me. I put my tapedeck on top
of my roommate's desk. I place my tape boxes on the floor to the
right of the comfy chair. I slip in a tape: bluegrass--good for
road trips and writing. I turn my new fridgie about 90° so that I
have ready access to the goodies inside. I pull Joe over. Joe is a
lamp. God knows why my roommate named his light "Joe." My roommate
also likes Black Sabbath. He is also a redhead. He is from Long Is-
land (pronounced lon-gi-land). I suspect these facts are inter-
related.

I steal a shelf from my roommate and lay it across the arms of
the chair. It is, I find, a better desk than my lap.

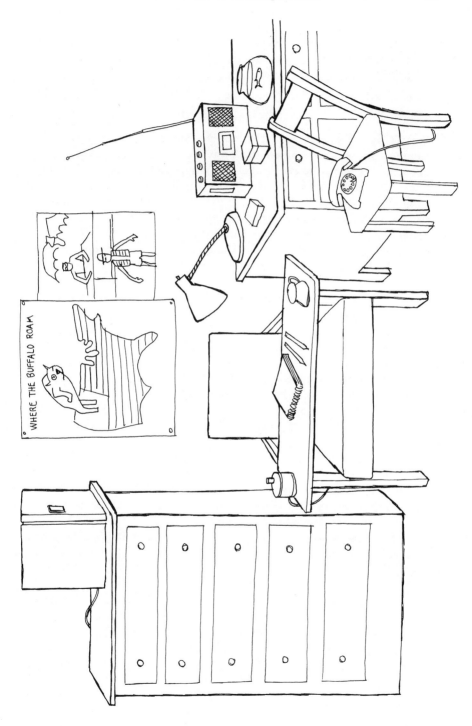

I am now ready to write. I commence at 8:00 p.m. The phone
rings at 8:45 p.m. It is Barb calling collect from Vermont. We talk
until 9:15 p.m. (see diagram).

NO/	TIME/	PLACE	NUMBER	/MIN/	CHARGE
1	845p	BURLINGTON VT	802 6564421	31	10.27

At 9:30 p.m. I get hungry and focus my attention on some Dannon All-
Natural Strawberry Yogurt with active yogurt cultures. I am at
first leery about having active yogurts in my tummy, but what the
hell--it can be no worse than the cafeteria food around here. I re-
sume writing at 9:45 p.m. At 10:20 p.m. my next-door neighbor Susan comes in and complains about "how weird Matt is." I
understand. Matt meditates in his closet with scented candles and
says things like "out in the lithosphere" at inappropriate times.
Susan leaves shortly after 11:00 p.m. I write for another half an
hour when my roommate walks in.

"I had to give my brother Jimmy his turntable back for a
while," he says.

"Bummer," I say, secretly gleeful--no Black Sabbath for
days, maybe even weeks!

My roommate goes to bed. It is now 12:05 a.m. Someone screams
into the airshaft outside my window, "I'm mad as hell and I'm not
going to take it anymore!" He repeats the call twice. He is answered by several angry (recently awakened) people who reply with
things like, "Quiet!" and, "Hold it down!" and, "Shut up!" There
is no further shouting.

It is 12:15 a.m. I start writing my English essay. I do my best
work at night, not necessarily because it's night, but because I
do my best work when under pressure. I am under pressure because I
have to get enough sleep to be semi-coherent the next morning. If
it weren't for all those damned distractions! I lament . . .

But then again, I don't mind . . ., where else would I get my
material?

Flow

The process I use when I write is simply to write. Once I have a
satisfactory first paragraph (which may take as many as six or
seven rewrites before it's acceptable), my writing follows a sort
of stream-of-consciousness sequence. It doesn't always turn out
to be a logical sequence, but I almost always get a sequence that
flows.

I feel that in my 19 years I have successfully mastered the
English language and therefore am now allowed to play with it any

way I want to. Which I do. I love playing with word combinations, delight in playing with persona, literary devices, points of view and styles.

I like to make the reader participate. Will she notice the southern baptist minister in this passage? Will she recognize the quote from "White Heat" in this essay? Will she try to figure out who "J. Litvinas" is? Writing should be a wonder-full travel through the author's mind.

The very paper my essays are written on are part of the essay. "Wonder-full" when read aloud will come out as "wonderful" and thus lose its impact. Visual games (pens (✓)) are lost. Diagrams are too tough to vocally explain. Writing is by nature visual, and if I can take it one step beyond that, then I'll feel as if I've accomplished something.

I have only two rules for writing:
1. It is a sin to be boring.
2. Writing should be a r
           a
         i
           n
            b
             o
              w

Interactions

- What aspect of his writing process has Brian focused on? List some ways that his description of his writing process differs from Lance's.
- Brian procrastinates. In other words, Brian puts off writing. Interview two class members in order to find out if they put off writing. If they do, what strategies do they use to procrastinate? If not, what are their reasons for starting early? How do they spend their time? Write a paper in which you argue for or against putting off writing, using the interviews, your own experiences, and the writing process papers in this chapter as your evidence.
- Write a description of the environment which for you is most conducive to writing. You may want to refer back to your response to Question 6 of your writing profile. Read your description to your writing group. What does your description have in common with those of other members of your group?

□   □   □

David Bogoslaw, another good student writer, talks about his writing process in a different way. What does his writing process have in common with Brian's?

A WRITER'S PENANCE

David Bogoslaw

There has been something about the winter in past years that has spurred me to write more than other seasons have. Perhaps it's been the weather, which keeps me awake and inside most of the time. Possibly it has been the schedule that school imposes on a student. Most likely it is a combination of the two. The paradox is that my largest body of work and from that my best work has been created of a winter, and yet it is during that period that I have the least amount of time to give to writing. Thus I am caught: having the need and wanting to write, but faced with a dearth of time. That may be the clue to my creative bursts, that they come only when I know I should be doing something else.

On days when there was no afterschool activity to keep me past two-thirty, I would ride the bus from school, anxious to get home and listen to Christmas carols and popular seasonal songs on the radio. I frequently had a writing project in progress. Nothing was more satisfying than a story or a play with a Christmas setting. Christmas settings seemed to set their own mood and that made the writing much less difficult. Music provided a mood better than anything else could, and so my brother and mother would return to find me listening to yuletide corn in preparation for another writing session on a gray afternoon.

For two years a screenplay called The Christmas Incident was the reason for such an odd approach to writing. A mystery-comedy set in early December, it depended on a prewriting mood more than a prose story would have. It was mostly dialogue and thus, I did not have the chance to create mood as much through description and background. After a more-than-adequate snack and some thirty minutes of "Hark the Herald Angels Sing" and the like, I would retire to my bedroom, where I'd read over a scene I was working on, look at notes I had made on characters and plot, and begin typing.

Now typing, the reader is asked to understand, works well for dialogue, but impedes the thought of a writer engulfed in prose. Well, it impeded this writer. Prose is a quiet, thoughtful kind of writing, while dialogue is merely people speaking and can withstand the pounding of typewriter keys. Wording and rhythm are important in both, the latter especially in writing comedy, but I demand the unobtrusive pen in creating description and narrative.

During my writing sessions of The Christmas Incident, which I still hope to return to one of these winters, I would sit on an old, non-working, console stereo given me by my grandparents, a type-writer at a comfortable angle before me on a table. The rest of the table was usually cluttered with old versions of a particular scene and notes, which were shuffled about constantly. Song lyrics on scraps of paper also were part of the clutter, for boredom brought a need to write lyrics to favorite songs. A cluttered desk made me feel more comfortable, as did a sheet of paper in the type-writer with occasional words or entire lines crossed out on it. A lack of neatness and apparent order dismissed the serious intent that often accompanied my writing sessions. I didn't want to feel that what I was writing had to be worth reading later. The fact that there were typing errors and obliterated changed thoughts further convinced me that imperfection didn't matter in the end.

Those things that characterized my writing process then still apply now. Mood is nearly all I will think about before writing a paper, because mood directly affects diction and sentence structure. Hence, structure of thought and portrayal of theme are influenced too by mood. The first sentence of a piece of writing, essay or story, causes me much anxiety. Although theme and argument are certainly important, the way I write interests me more. All a writer has, finally, is his style, his way of stating a point, of linking words and creating images. The latter is mandatory, for writing should be a series of images. If it doesn't sound like good writing to me, it probably isn't, and I can get quite discouraged with a piece. Because I approach essay-writing as I do story-writing, I can wait for an idea on how to begin an essay nearly as long as for the subject of a story. The factor that hurries me with an essay is the deadline that I must meet.

The fact that I have a three-draft process to use in creating a paper this year does not lessen the anxiety of setting pen to paper. There is something that makes me believe that sloppiness in diction leads to sloppiness of thought. My feeling is why write even the first draft if one had no definite plan for diction and arrangement that a first sentence can suggest. This, of course, is silly, because the airing of ideas is the primary purpose of a paper and a style of wording can come from that. Only in dialogue can I write randomly, to the point where each line a character says is a revelation to me. Otherwise, I feel I must know my plan of attack before I leave the base. I can sit, think, and drift for hours, waiting for a phrase to occur that will send me to write, a dangerously slow process.

Music still establishes a mood from which I can draw plans for a paper. Different kinds of music work for different stories, or

subjects. Pieces with Christmas background demand carols and
snow songs. Lately, because my essays have drawn from past experience, I have relied on mellow rock or folk to make me more reflective. Music is an interesting device for setting a mood for
writing. There are so many associations people have with music in
their lives that a particular piece can send one back to a party, a
car trip, or a whole summer. Another piece of writing can trigger
certain feelings and thoughts, too, and sometimes reaffirm a
thought considered before, but not developed. I will read someone's writing for thought, for language, or just for distraction
to clear my mind. Often I lie on my bed thinking and remembering,
but that rarely spurs me to write. When nothing else works and a
deadline is near, I attempt nonsense: writing something devoid of
coherence, with inappropriate adjectives and multi-syllabic
names. Nonsense can jar the jumble from my mind at times.

But when that phrase I needed does occur, or an overall plan
for a paper becomes apparent, I come to a cluttered desk and begin.
A pen is usually the chosen instrument, but in my less certain moments, I substitute a pencil. There is friction between lead and
paper that isn't there with a pen; writing becomes slower and allows me more time to think. The chair is pulled back a good space
from the desk and I lean forward over my paper, which is placed at a
slant on the desk. Before beginning, I try to be neat, with combed
hair and sleeves comfortable about my arms. Whether the writing
proceeds smoothly or not, though, I rely on nervous habits to ensure my sanity. Nail-biting and running fingers through hair are
almost unconscious, but are frequent, and I rock my legs back and
forth, too. The writing session is not always without pauses. I
may look up a word in the thesaurus, listen to a song on an album, or
break to eat. When a paper has gone well, I am sorry to have to finish it. But when it's been a painful birth, I grow hasty toward the
end and am relieved to rest my hand.

Second and third drafts usually come more easily than the
first. After reading all previous drafts, I think of what I want
changed and the fact that I have a finished paper before me is comfort enough when trying to improve it. The problem is that I'm reluctant to cut a favorite phrase or passage that may be unneeded or
unclear. Conclusions, too, bother me, for I must try hard to avoid
being pat and formally conclusive. Subject and theme, having already been established, are shelved and I concentrate totally on
diction. I can complete a second or third draft while a stereo or
television is on, but if I reach a snag in logic or language, I need
quiet again to think out a new tack. When reading over a paper at
completion or much later, I can be satisfied only when I am re-

turned to the mood in which the piece was originally written. If the mood doesn't return, the paper is not as good as it should be, or I have more pressing matters on my mind, such as the next assignment.

Interactions

- Discuss in your group what David's attitudes and feelings about writing are. Make a list of what you, David, Brian, and Kathryn Lance share as writers. On the basis of this list, what generalizations can you make about good writers, both student and professional?
- What advice about writing would you give now to anyone entering a writing class?

□   □   □

The value of listening to writers talking about the way they write is that you can find out that not all writers work in the same way, although they do share certain attitudes about writing and use similar strategies to make their writing more effective. By looking closely at the way good writers work, you become aware of how your writing process is similar or different.

When you are conscious of what you're doing as a writer, you can examine, evaluate, and possibly change it. What you must first become aware of is the choices you're making as a writer and the strategies available to you.

□   □   □

Writing-and-Revising Two

(a) Write a paper in which you discuss your own writing process in as much detail as possible. To gather material for your paper, you may want to review your responses to the Interactions in this chapter and your answers to the questionnaire in Chapter 1. You may also want to examine drafts of a piece of your writing to see what kinds of changes you made. And you may want to explore further your history as a writer to see what has influenced your development. Save all notes and drafts so that you can refer to them from time to time.

(b) Interview a person who is currently working in a field that interests you, perhaps one you would like to enter. Ask him or her the questions provided in the Writing Profile Questionnaire. Find out what kinds of writing he or she does. Is writing important in the job? Ask the person about his or her experiences with writing in school. Are these experiences similar to yours? Does this person need a certain environment in which to write? Does the person have time to share his or her writing with colleagues?

Write a paper discussing the person's writing process.

(c) Interview a published writer—for example, a columnist for your local newspaper, a professor, an advertising copywriter, a song lyricist, a poet. Ask your subject to talk about his or her experiences as a writer. You may want to use questions from the Writing Profile Questionnaire.

Write a paper discussing the writing process of the writer you interviewed. Include your own response to what you find out.

(d) Interview someone much younger than you are—for example, a student in elementary school. Ask your subject to describe how he or she goes about writing.

Write a paper in which you develop the profile of the person you interviewed.

Cat got your pencil?

Chapter 3

The Choices Writers Make

An artist observes, selects, guesses, and combines.

ANTON CHEKHOV

Writing-and-revising is the process of selecting, ordering, questioning, and changing. When you write, you make preliminary decisions about what you're going to say and in what order you're going to say it based on your sense of the best way to say things to accomplish your purpose and meet the needs of your reader. By making these choices, you're continually discovering new ideas and new ways to express them.

As you select and order, however, you're also questioning your choices and often changing them. Sometimes you question immediately. You select one idea and before you begin to write you decide that it just won't work. Or you may write something down and realize instantly that this is not what you wanted to say and then cross it out. At other times you realize that your initial plan for ordering what you're writing is no longer appropriate; what you thought you wanted to say is not what you now want to say. At other times you must write out your entire initial selection and ordering to see where it takes you. Then you stop and question whether this is indeed what you want to say and if your reader will understand what you mean.

Where do the questions come from? They come from your trying to discover what you want to say. They also come from your awareness of the relationship between what you want to say and what you have actually said. And they come from your sense of how you want your reader to respond and how you feel he or she will actually respond to what you've written.

How do you change your work? There are several possible ways. You may delete ideas or language, substitute ideas or words, reorder words and ideas, add material to your initial selection when you feel it's appropriate to your purpose and audience. This process of selecting, ordering, questioning, and changing is what you do as you write and revise. Thus, writing-and-revising is one process, the act of repeatedly making choices.

There isn't, however, any formula to follow or any set number of strategies that you can use in order to make your writing better automatically. Writing-and-revising comes about because writers have something to say and have a sense that the way they're saying it doesn't convey their intended meaning. This "sense" is something that writers develop by interacting with readers or by distancing themselves from their writing by becoming readers of their own texts.

The biggest temptation for all writers is to become satisfied too quickly with what they've written. As one experienced writer in Chapter 1 noted, "My cardinal rule ... is never to fall in love with what I have written in a first or second draft. An idea, sentence, or even a phrase that looks catchy—I don't trust. Part of this idea is to wait awhile. I am much more in love with something after I have written it than I am a day or two later." And as another writer explained, "It is a matter of looking at the kernel of what I have written, the content, and then thinking about it, responding to it, making decisions, and actually restructuring." Writing-and-revising strategies, then, are ways of reformulating and re-envisioning what you've written. The strategies depend on your being tentative about your decisions so that you can find out what you want to say and how you want to say it.

Stephanie Oppenheim, a student writer, wrote an autobiographical sketch in which she attempted to convey certain memories of her childhood. In her first draft, she chose a particular incident to describe. What we don't know and can't know is what motivated all the choices she made in writing the first draft. But we do have her second draft of the episode, and we can at least speculate about what choices she made in revising the piece.

Interactions

• In writing-and-revising, Stephanie selected new material to include in her essay. As you read her first draft, locate several places where she could add new material and, in the margin, explain why you'd want her to do so.

□   □   □

<u>THE</u> <u>FIELD</u>

Stephanie Oppenheim

1)   Childhood memories often become blurred with time, but my memories of going berrypicking with my grandpa will always be clear and distinct. I will always remember that the second week of August meant I would have my grandpa to myself. In fact, this was one of the few times, when I was little, that we spent time together, alone.

2)   Under the hot summer sun, we would enter the fields with our long sleeves and pants ready to pick berries. Sometimes the ground was wet and made a soft crunchy and squeaky noise underneath my new sneakers. The bushes were sparkling green from the heavy rain the night before. Everything smelled so clean and fresh.

3)   Grandpa protected me from the thorny blackberry bushes and the snakes my mother always spoke about. I felt safe. He used to bring down the higher bushes to my height so I could pick the "best" berries. On a normal afternoon we probably ate twice as much as we put in the bucket to take home. We would make a pact not to eat any berries for five minutes, but the sweet smelling aroma always overcame us soon after we made the agreement.

4)   I used to laugh at how blue our tongues used to be. There was something very special about the sweet and sour taste of the summer's first berries. We ate so many at once that when dinner came around we were always covered with blue, scratched from the thorns, and too full to eat, much less look at another berry. Yet we were always ready by the next afternoon to start all over again.

5)   At least once I would trip and drop my berries; but Grandpa just grinned and gave me some more of his. He always managed to go berry picking in his new pants which were always snagged by the time we were done. His eyes used to smile, and I used to giggle, because we knew Grandma would ask him, as she did every year, why he went into the fields with his new pants.

6)   To many these afternoons might have seemed very quiet and dull; but he taught me how to listen for the beautiful music of the birds, who ate and sang above us, the rustling of the rabbits as we approached, and the buzzing bees that meant that there were good berries just around the corner.

7)   This summer I walked to the field, with Anna, a seven year old from down the road; yet I was very much alone. I was no longer alone with my grandpa. Now I was the protector, the bush lowerer. All afternoon I wondered how Anna would remember this day, if she would at all, if she would remember the scratchy noises of the blackberry bushes or the sensation of looking up into the bushes and seeing the sun shine through.

8)   Anna and I were picking berries together when I remembered
how whenever I heard a noise Grandpa could be sure I'd be right behind him, holding onto him tightly. My mind kept drifting back to
the past, expecting my grandpa to be there when I looked up. Anna
was my reminder that things were no longer the same. I felt like
crying, but being here was an important test. Grandpa was still
with me, in a different way, and I was still his little girl.

9)   The sun still felt as warm as ever, our hands were still
sticky and blue from holding the berries in our hands, and the
birds' melody was as clear and cheerful as it had always been. I was
picking berries, thinking back to the countless summers I spent
here happily with my grandpa, when Anna was frightened by the sudden movement of a rabbit. My memories I knew would always be with
me. Those afternoons with my grandpa gave me a chance to become his
friend. My friendship with my grandpa continued to grow, and we
began to talk and learn more about each other as I got older. The
bond we made together will always be with me. I know that now. It
was time for me to show and share the wonders of nature to another
the way he showed me. I took Anna's hand and we walked home, together.

Interactions

• Compare your suggestions of where Stephanie could add material to
her essay with those of the other members of your writing group. List
all the points in the text where additions could be made and note the
reasons for these additions given by your group.

☐ ☐ ☐

Keeping her first six paragraphs essentially unchanged, Stephanie made substantial changes in her paper beginning with paragraph
seven. Read her second draft beginning with paragraph six and note
what changes she did indeed make.

☐ ☐ ☐

6)   To many these afternoons might have seemed very quiet and
dull; but he taught me how to listen for the beautiful music of the
birds, who ate and sang above us, the rustling of the rabbits as we
approached and the buzzing bees that meant there were good berries
just around the corner.

7)   I sat outside this summer with my back to the field. I missed
Grandpa, his death still didn't seem real. Every time I heard a car

door shut my heart raced, Grandpa--it couldn't be--I felt sick, the knot in my throat got larger. I avoided going berry picking, it wouldn't be the same. I felt so empty inside, his smiling eyes, his teasing words, where do I put them? Everything went dark.

"Guess who?" a small voice asked which matched the tiny hands that covered my eyes.

"Wonder Woman?" I asked knowing it was Anna, a seven year old from down the road.

"No," she giggled giving me a hug. "It's me, Anna. Stephanie what's in the field over there?"

"Berries," I said, knowing where this conversation was leading me.

"Berries! Take me, Stephanie, please, what kind of berries? I love berries, Stephanie!" she said in an excited rush.

"Blueberries and the best blackberries in the county." It was time, I thought to myself, time to face the field. "O.K., Anna, let's go get buckets."

We walked to the field together, yet I was very much alone. I was no longer alone with my grandpa. Now I was the protector, the one to pull the bush lower. All afternoon I wondered how Anna would remember this day, if she would at all, if she would remember the scratchy noises of the blackberry bushes or the sensation of looking up into the bushes and seeing the sun struggling to shine through.

Anna and I were picking berries together when I remembered how whenever I heard a noise Grandpa could be sure I'd be right behind him holding onto him tightly. My mind kept drifting back to the past, expecting my grandpa to be there when I looked up. Anna was my reminder that things were no longer the same. I felt like crying; but being here was an important test. Grandpa was still with me, in a different way, and I was still his little girl.

The sun still felt as warm as ever, our hands were still sticky and blue from holding the berries in our hands, and the birds' melody was as clear and cheerful as it had always been. I was picking berries, thinking back to the countless summers I spent here happily with my Grandpa, when Anna was frightened by the sudden movement of a rabbit. She held on tightly. My memories I knew would always be with me. Those afternoons with my grandpa gave me a chance to become his friend. My friendship with Grandpa continued to grow, and we began to talk and learn more about each other as I got older. The bond we made together will always be with me; I know that now. It was time for me to show and share the wonders of nature to another the way he showed me. I took Anna's hand and we walked home, together.

Interactions

- Did any of Stephanie's additions correspond to the ones you or your group had indicated?
- Speculate about what motivated Stephanie to change her piece as she did. What questions do you suppose she might have asked herself in the process of making these choices?
- Write your own account of a childhood memory. Read this draft to your writing group and ask them if anything needs to be added.

  Rewrite your account. Share it with your writing group and explain your writing-and-revising strategy. What further changes would you like to make?

  Write a final draft. Before you present the entire piece to your writing group, read only the first paragraph. Ask them to tell you what they're anticipating from hearing the first paragraph. Then read the entire paper. Were their speculations correct? If not, does it make a difference? Why or why not? (You may want to revise your piece further in order to meet the needs of your readers.)

□   □   □

The process of selecting and ordering determines what you say and how you say it. This process, therefore, limits temporarily other things you could say and other ways of ordering. Often, in subsequent drafts, writers will change the order of presentation and by so doing discover new things to say. For example, Tim Tseng, a student writer, tells a story about his grandfather which is strikingly different from Stephanie's essay.

Interactions

- As you read the first draft of Tim's essay, write in the margin a one-sentence summary of what each paragraph says.

□   □   □

Last Chinese New Year, our family gathered together in the living room to celebrate after a special dinner. In accordance to Chinese tradition, the eldest member of the household would have all attention focused on him as he told stories of the family's past. In our home, no one washed the dishes after dinner. We were together singing hymns, making prayers, and studying the Bible. After that was done, my younger brothers and I sprawled over the living room carpet focusing all our attention on father. What

would he talk about tonight? Grandfather? Great-grandfather? Or
his experiences when he converted to Christianity? Mother sat
next to father knitting his sweater. She listened intently to father as he revealed some wonderfully mysterious secrets. That
night he revealed to us about a time of great suffering when he was
a child of seven or eight.

   When I was a child, I never experienced the sufferings my father did when he was a child. In 1936, a great famine hit Southwestern China. Kweichow, my father's home province, was one of several
provinces to suffer such misery. It was reported that nearly fifteen million Chinese peasants and farmers died of starvation. Father vividly recalls seeing strong men collapse to their deaths in
the middle of their tracks. People everywhere were suffering--
some just gave up all hope. Grandfather, the Mayor of Wuchuan
County, worked ceaselessly to help them and even sacrificed his
own family's meals quite often in order to help hungry neighbors.
Father lived on two small meals a day and was extremely thin in
those days. Father often spoke with pride about how much care
grandfather showed towards fellow impoverished Chinese. Although grandfather's family was relatively well off before the
famine, after it, the family was left penniless.

   Great-grandfather was a renowned poet before the famine and
had memorized all of the Chinese classics. During the famine, he
gave up poetry temporarily in order to help the needy, though he
was so old that he could hardly walk.

   The great famine of 1936 began in 1935 when all the provinces
in Southwestern China were flooded. The Wu Yiang River, which
passed through Wuchuan Province, overflowed and destroyed many
crops. Unusual droughts followed the flood and wiped out even more
crops. By April of 1936, millions of Chinese people were dying of
starvation. To make matters worse, Chinese Communist soldiers
swept through Kweichow and its surrounding provinces and took any
remaining food from the peasants. Cannibalism was found in the
worst affected area. The beautiful green mountains Kweichow was
famous for were stripped of all their leaves. Its trees were
stripped of their barks as hunger-crazed Chinese became desper-
ate. Dogs and cats were devoured; suicide increased. There seemed
to be no end in sight and General Chiang Kai-shek could do nothing
about it.

   This period proved to be very traumatic for father. Witness-
ing so much human suffering at such a young age and experiencing it
made him the way he is today. As father continues his story of how
his family survived the famine without much loss, one could tell
that father and grandfather had great strength and courage and
most importantly, concern for fellow humans.

By now, my youngest brother was asleep, the other brother
just about to fall asleep. Mother was tired too; it was 2:30 a.m.
Me? Well I was fascinated and so grateful that father was able to
tell us a little more about himself and his past. All throughout
his life, my father's been helping the poor and impoverished. I
believe his decision to join the ministry was motivated by the
fact that his concern for the less fortunate was so great. As we
prepared to sleep that night, a night to be remembered, pride in my
father's accomplishments and respect for his experience grew
greatly within me. I hoped that I would never experience what he
suffered through, but also hoped that I would be able to help those
who are suffering right now.

Interactions

- As you read Tim's second draft, once again write in the margin a one-
  sentence summary of each paragraph.

□   □   □

WUCHUAN COUNTY, 1936

Timothy Tseng

Their bark stripped, leaves all gone, the trees in Kweichow
Province in Southwest China looked gloomy and frightening. The
once lovely green mountains which made Kweichow famous became a
solemn grayish-brown. The forests were unusually quiet--no birds
chirped, no rustling of leaves and grass caused by the movements
of running hares. Just below the mountains lay a desolate valley.
Once full of vigor and life, the River Wu Yiang had shrunken down to
nothing more than a brook. The sand that formerly was the bank of
the great river became scorchingly white, and just beyond it, the
meadowgrass browned. A few miles down the river, one could see a
small mud-hut with a large field behind it. As we neared the hut, we
could see the sun beaten soil ruined by flood erosion and drought.
Little remains of the noticeably disastrous harvest lay scattered around the field. Inside the hut, there came a sound, a sound
of a child crying.[1]

In the middle of the floor sat a skinny slanted-eyed baby. She
cried, her stomach ached from starvation. She was frightened because her dead parents would not move. The parents were also bony
and their bodies were beginning to decompose and smell. Several
bullet holes could be seen on both of their chests. Apparently,
Chinese Communists,[2] also starved due to the famine, came in the
hut, raided them of all their food, and shot both parents when they

attempted to put up a struggle. As the girl of about three continued whimpering, footsteps from the south approached the hut. A
team of five men rushed into the hut and tended to the child, giving
her food, and they later buried her parents. A few moments after-
wards, the senior member of the team brought the child back towards the south to his home while the others continued the search
for any other survivors.

He carried the child into the outskirts of the major village
in Wuchuan County and brought her to a hospital sponsored by the
China International Famine Relief Commission[3] so they could take
better care of the child.

"Isn't she lovely, Mayor Tseng?" asked the short but soft-
eyed receptionist.

"She certainly is. Horrendous that her parents were mur-
dered."

After the transaction, the Mayor returned to his home. He
lived a few miles away from the village in a wooden house (which was
slightly better than a mud-hut). Inside, he wished that he had
something else to wear. What he and his family wore now were en-
trenched with the stench of perspiration, flesh, and soil. He
couldn't wash the clothing now, the drought had dried up so much of
the water supply. Right now, what would be more relaxing than a
pipe of opium and a few bedtime stories with "Lou-er" (second eldest son)? He is writing poetry right now--only seven--how bril-
liant, his grandfather has taught him well. What a painful memory
the Mayor felt when he remembered how his eldest son fell victim to
the great famine that began the previous year, 1935.

Last year, the dreadful flooding of the Wu Yiang River caused
serious damage to the crops. As a result many people died of starvation if not by drowning. Thank goodness most of his family survived the flood. But now, it was worse. It hadn't rained for months
and all the crops were ruined. How would anyone survive this famine created by these disasters? Some have already given up and
committed suicide after finding no more dogs, cats, rabbits,
rats, or snakes left for food. They refused to become cannibals
and as a result were eaten by their own relatives after their suicide. A few neighbors have sold their wives and children just to
receive a little food. After a while, when they had nothing left at
all, they too killed themselves.[4]

"But no more. Must put away all unpleasant thoughts," thought
the Mayor. "The family will survive though the odds are against it
and 'Lou-er' will go on to tell his sons about what he went
through."

Mayor Tseng put the pipe in his mouth, lit the opium, smoked a
few breaths, and felt good.

At that moment over fifteen million people in Southwest China died or were dying of starvation as Japanese troops marched into the Northern parts of China. General Chiang Kai-shek's arms were tied and could do nothing about the famine.[5] Those horrifying days were a vivid reality to my father.

My grandfather, Mayor Tseng, was a strong and gifted leader. He wanted to make sure that all his children would be educated though there was a famine and though he knew that he could never afford the costs of education. Luckily, Great-grandfather was a master of poetry and taught my father (Lou-er) many of the great Chinese Classics. As my father told that story, his mind was wandering somewhere, recalling vividly his childhood memories. Our family sat in the living room as he spoke. My brothers and I sprawled over the carpet--Steven, the youngest child, was asleep and Paul, the middle, was half asleep. Mother was busy knitting and only paid partial attention to father. Only me and my father were letting our minds roam around in the past.

Notes

1. "China Fears 15,000,000 Deaths in Famines; Vast Szechwan Province Has No Food," New York Times, 20 April 1936, Sec. A, p. 8, col. 2.
2. "China Fears 15,000,000 Deaths . . . ," p. 8.
3. "Annual Report of the Kweichow Provincial Committee of the China International Famine Relief Commission for 1935," China International Famine Relief Commission Report, 1936, p. 84.
4. "Famine in China," Literary Digest, 9 May 1936, p. 16.
5. George Moseley, China Since 1911 (New York: Harper and Row, 1968), pp. 58-60.

Bibliography

"Annual Report of the Kweichow Provincial Committee of the China International Famine Relief Commission for 1935." China International Famine Relief Commission Report, 1936, p. 84.

"China Fears 15,000,000 Deaths in Famine; Vast Szechwan Province Area Has No Food." New York Times, 20 April 1936, Sec. A, p. 8, col. 2.

"Famine in China." Literary Digest, 9 May 1936, p. 16.

Moseley, George. China Since 1911. New York: Harper and Row, 1968.

Interactions

- Compare your paragraph-by-paragraph summaries of Tim's two drafts. How has the order of events changed? What effect does this re-ordering have on you as a reader?
- Determine what new information was added to the second draft. What information appeared in the first draft but not in the second?
- In each draft of Tim's essay, try to figure out who is telling the story in each paragraph—that is, who is the narrator. How does the focus of the story change in the second draft?
- Compare paragraph four in the first draft with paragraph one in the second draft. In both paragraphs, Tim gives the same information. What changes has he made to create a different effect in the second version?
- Make a list of questions Tim might have asked himself in the process of writing-and-revising.
- Write your own version of a story from your family or neighborhood. Share your first draft with your writing group and ask them to write a one-sentence summary of each paragraph.

  Rewrite your story and share it with your writing group, having each member also write a one-sentence summary of each paragraph. Now compare the two drafts, together with the summaries for each. What has changed from draft to draft? The order of events? The focus of your story?

  Ask your writing group to suggest writing-and-revising strategies to help you bring your story into final form. Then share your final product and discuss the changes you made.

□ □ □

A piece of writing can go through many drafts before the writer feels that it's finished. However, the basic structure of a paper may be apparent from the beginning. To see how this works, read the following story by Sara Lewis, a student writer, presented here in its first draft.

I had worked until 4:00 that morning. At 7:30 I was not ready to receive phone calls. In fact the phone rang three times before I figured out what that sound was. He was here, he said, at the bus station.

"Didn't Mom call you?" he asked. She had not.

"Don't you have school? Is this vacation or something?"

"Got suspended for reefin' out. I had to leave, go somewhere and ponder my actions. I'm staying with you for a few days."

"Okay. Come on down. Only knock really loud when you get here. I'm going back to bed."

At one that afternoon, my brother was cooking us breakfast. I
had not had refried beans on flour tortillas for a long time. The
warm, oily, slightly heavy smell reminded me of cozier times and
places. We sat down on the couch to eat as I didn't have a table.

"I couldn't find a good avocado," he said. "They're all from
Florida. Thin-skinned and watery. I decided we'd be better off
without it. Listen, I don't mean to get personal, but where's David?"

"Didn't Mom tell you? He's gone. I threw him out. Well, not
really. We both sort of felt it was necessary."

"That's why you're so thin?"

"I'm always thin. Yeah, I guess. For the first week I barfed
every day. I lost 10 pounds. Now here I am eating refried beans for
breakfast. Progress."

"Bummer."

"Really."

For a second I thought I might throw up again, but I overcame
it, and we ate our beans in silence. I had a hard time adjusting to
the way he looked. My brother had had long hair since he was twelve.
That was the year our father had died. Our father was the only one
opposed to long hair. The rest of us thought long hair was okay, so
my brother when he was 17, his hair was to his waist. Now half a year
later it was gone. He had cut it within a half inch of his scalp. Red
hair, though it can be very beautiful, brings along all sorts of
other problems. My brother had them all: he sunburned in minutes--
at home he had been an avid surfer and had to cover himself with
layers of sun lotion several times a day at the beach; he had thousands of freckles; he had a tendency to look too pink. That is, his
skin had a pinkish tone and his lips were dark red. If he weren't
feeling extremely confident he looked pink and vulnerable. Not
vulnerable like a kitten, but vulnerable like a newly hatched
bird. He had this look now. The haircut accentuated this rather
hungry abandoned look. That is why I decided not to mention it
right away.

"I was doing really good but I blew it. Crashed and burned. I
hadn't toked since I went up there. You know, they have this honor
code. You all agree not to smoke dope while you go to school there.
And you agree that if you do see someone doing it you'll report them
to the rest of the group. This one time I felt like toking, this guy
sees me like he didn't even tell me he saw me. Just stood up at Friday Night meeting and told everyone. This other guy got suspended.
He was with me. He smoked too. I feel like such a little fool. Why
did I do it? Like last year at Granger High I know why I did it; I
couldn't stand that stinking hole. So I smoked and never went to
class. No great loss. But now, up at Vermont Outlook, like it's

really cool. Like you're in rapture. And you work in the community
like now we're trying to stop a nuclear power plant from being
built. I have this really cool girlfriend, Joanne. She's really
smart and she's teaching me about marine biology. But now I did
this and they all know it. I'm really sorry I did it. It's different
than before. I feel like I let them down."

I didn't feel I could be of much help.

Interactions

- Make a list of the facts you know about the two principal characters
  from reading the first draft.
- Write a draft of a character sketch describing the brother.

◻ ◻ ◻

Now read the second draft.

I had worked until four that morning. At seven-thirty, I was
not ready to receive a phone call. In fact, the phone had rung three
times before I figured out what that sound was. On the sixth ring, I
answered it. It was my brother Finch. He was here, he said, at the
bus station.

"Didn't Mom call you?" She had not.

"Don't you have school? This isn't a vacation, is it?" I was
having a lot of trouble assembling the facts.

"Got suspended for smoking dope. I had to leave, go somewhere
and ponder my actions. I'm staying with you for a few days."

"Oh. Okay. But when you get here, knock loud. I'm going back
to bed."

I had a hard time adjusting to the way he looked. My brother
had had long hair since he was eleven. That was the year our father
had died. Our father had been the only one of us opposed to long
hair. So, at eleven, Finch stopped cutting it, except for biannual
trims. By the time he was seventeen, his hair had grown to his
waist. Now, half a year later, it was almost entirely gone. He had
had it cut to within an inch of his scalp. Red hair, though it can be
very beautiful, can bring with it many problems. My brother has
them all: He sunburns in minutes (at home, he had been an avid surfer and had to keep covering himself with layers of protective lotions all day at the beach); he has thousands of freckles; he
blushes easily; cold, heat, and spicy food make him turn very red.
He has a tendency to look too pink. The slightest sign of trouble
causes a deepening of his natural pinkness. When he is feeling
rather cocky, he is quite handsome. But when he has suffered some

defeat, he looks pink and vulnerable. It is not the cute vulnerability of a kitten, but rather the vulnerability of a baby bird.
His drastic new haircut accentuated this hungry, abandoned look.
I decided that mentioning the haircut would be a big mistake right
now.

At one that afternoon, my brother was cooking breakfast. I
had not had a bean burrito in a long time. I hadn't even found a
place to buy refried beans since I moved here. The warm, slightly
oily smell of the beans reminded me of a more secure, easier time.

"I couldn't find a good avocado," Finch said. "They're all
from Florida. Thin-skinned and watery." He thoughtfully licked
the spoon, then stuck it back in the beans and resumed his stirring. "Listen," he said, "I don't mean to get personal, but like,
where's David?"

"Didn't Mom tell you? He's gone. We decided it was really important that he have his own space to bring his girlfriends home
to. I'm sure you've heard how important it is to have your own
space."

Finch was now studying me. I both dreaded and looked forward
to his next comment. "You're really skinny, Lucy. You lose all
this weight since he left?"

"What do you mean? I'm always thin." I don't usually admit it,
but I can be a real martyr. "Yeah, I guess that's why. The first
week after he left, I barfed everyday. Every time I thought about
moving all the way here to live with that turd, it made me sick. I
lost ten pounds. Now, two weeks later, here I am eating refried
beans for breakfast. Progress."

"Bummer."

"Really."

We finished our beans in silence. Finch stared at his hiking
boots. Out of habit, he reached back to adjust his pony tail. As his
fingers closed on nothing, he blushed. I began to examine a plant
that was dying. Finch lit a Winston. He got up and sat on the radiator.

"I was doing really good," he said. "But I blew it. Crashed
and burned. I didn't think it would happen this time, but it did.
You know they have this honor code. You all agree not to smoke pot
while you go to school there. That way, I guess they figure it will
keep us all more together. We'll be a unit, like, so people won't
end up in cliques and stuff. I hadn't toked since I went up there.
Swear to God. This one day, this guy and me, we decided it would be
fun to do some smoke and go walk in the snow. This other guy saw us,
only we didn't know it. Two weeks later, he stands up in Friday
Night Meeting, and he reports it to the whole school. Like, I know I
deserved it, but I felt so humiliated.

"I am such a fool. At Granger High I smoked because I hated that stinking hole. I smoked and never went to school. Survival. The only way. But now, up at Vermont Outlook, it's different. It's the school I wanted to go to. You live and work with the community. And we're trying to help the locals stop a nuclear power plant from being built. I have this really cool girl friend, Joanne. She's twenty, and she's really smart, and she's teaching me marine biology. I was even thinking of taking the SAT's and trying to get into some college, but I blew it.

"They all voted that the two of us that smoked should go away from school for a while and think about whether we wanted to come back and renew our commitment. After the meeting, Joanne came over to my room. I was packing. She told me she was really disappointed in me. I'm not going back. This is not the first time I've done something like this, you know."

I knew. Finch had always had school problems. Even when things were going well, he seemed to almost deliberately get into trouble. The problem was that he didn't like school. It was that simple. I was tempted to tell him that it would all blow over, that it wasn't important, and that his friends were being melodramatic. But then, he could have told me that David had always been a jerk and that I was better off without him. Suffering is in the eye of the beholder. To Finch, his banishment was devastating. Once I grasped the enormity of it in Finch's estimation, I couldn't think of anything significant enough to say.

"What happened to your hair?" I asked.

"What do you think? I'm hiding it? I got it cut. After all this stuff happened, I was on the bus coming down here. I thought, 'I have nothing going for me. I'm just a big jerk.' I tried to think of just one good thing about myself. All I could come up with was my hair. I had to wait in Boston for three hours for the next bus. I was walking around and I saw this barber shop that was open. It was ten o'clock at night. Seemed like an omen to me. The barber's name was Wesley. Straightest guy I ever saw. He cut it. Took about three minutes. I think old Wesley really enjoyed himself. He called me Red. I was tempted not to tip him. But I didn't want that on my conscience, too. First time I been in a barber shop since I used to go with Dad. It still stunk."

Finch stayed with me for five days. I took a couple of days off work. We saw some movies and ate in a lot of restaurants. Finch found a black derby in perfect condition at an antique clothing store. He took me to a blues club that a boy at school had told him about. I was surprised that he knew quite a lot about the blues. It is always hard for me to understand that he can know things that I don't. I can remember teaching him how to swim underwater. But I

forget the several years that have passed since Finch and I lived
in the same town.

On the second day, he told me he was going to stay in the city.
He liked it much better here than the woods in Vermont. He was going
to stay and find work as a carpenter. I didn't say anything. By the
fourth day he wanted to call his friends at school. He talked for a
long time to several people. He used some words and phrases that I
had never heard. After the phone call, Finch lost the bereft look
that had hung over him since his arrival.

The next morning when I woke up, Finch was stuffing his
clothes into his backpack. He had written a two-page apology to
his classmates. He would read it the next night at Friday Night
Meeting. Everyone would forgive him.

Interactions

- Note that in the first draft, when Finch calls, he says he "got suspended for reefin' out" while in the second draft he says he "got suspended
  for smoking dope." Why do you suppose the author chose to make this
  change?
- In the second draft, the sequence of her story changes. The description
  of Finch, which originally followed the breakfast scene, comes first.
  What impact does this change have on you?
- In the second draft, the writer adds the sentence "He thoughtfully
  licked the spoon, then stuck it back in the beans and resumed his stirring." How does this affect you? How does it shape your sense of
  Finch's personality and habits?
- The first draft ends with the statement "I didn't feel I could be of
  much help." In the second draft, this statement becomes "I couldn't
  think of anything significant enough to say." How do the develop-
  ments that follow this statement change the shape of the story?
- Why do you think the writer might have selected new material about
  Finch?
- Revise your character sketch of Finch based on the new material in-
  troduced in the second draft.

□   □   □

The final draft of this piece has changed considerably from the
first draft, although it's still essentially the same story.

REFRIED BEANS

Sara Electra Lewis

In January of America's Bicentennial Year, the city was still unfamiliar to me. I was living alone and working at night. That morning, I had worked until four, and at seven-thirty I was not ready to receive a phone call. In fact, the phone had rung three times before I figured out what that sound was. I answered on the sixth ring. It was my brother Finch. He was here, he said, at the bus station.

"Didn't Mom call you?"

She had not. "Don't you have school? Is this a vacation, or something?" I was having a lot of trouble assembling the facts.

"Got suspended for smoking dope. I had to leave. Go somewhere and ponder my actions. I'm staying with you for a few days."

"Oh. Okay. But when you get here, knock loud, in case I fall asleep again."

I took the extra pillow off my bed and put it at one end of the couch. It was a long bus ride from Vermont to the city, and I figured Finch had been awake for most of it. Sheets and blankets were unnecessary, as my brother always travelled with a sleeping bag. I sat down in the kitchen on a straight-back chair to keep from falling asleep, but I feel asleep anyway. Finch knocked so loud, I jumped.

When I opened the door, I was quite startled by my brother's appearance. I had been right about the bus; Finch looked tired and disheveled. But I had certainly seen him look messier and more tired. What startled me was the fact that Finch's hair was cut to within an inch of his scalp. My brother had had long hair since he was eleven. That was the year our father had died. Our father had been the only one of us opposed to long hair. So, at eleven, Finch had stopped cutting his, except for semiannual trims. By the time he was seventeen, Finch's hair had grown to his waist. Now, half a year later, it was practically all gone. Because it was so short, it hardly looked like red hair anymore. His pink scalp showed through a little bit, and he looked as if he had an orange glow around his head.

Red hair, though it can be very beautiful, can bring with it many problems. My brother has them all. He sunburns in minutes (at home he had been an avid surfer, and all day at the beach he had to keep covering himself with protective lotions) ; he has thousands of freckles, he blushes easily, cold, heat and spicy food make him turn red very quickly. He has a tendency to look too pink. The slightest sign of trouble causes a deepening of his natural color. When he is feeling cocky, he can look quite handsome. But when he has suffered some defeat, he looks pink and vulnerable. It is not the cute vulnerability of a kitten, but rather the vulnerability of a newly hatched bird. This was the way he appeared to me now as he stepped into the kitchen. His drastic new haircut accentuated this hungry, abandoned look. Sleepy as I was, I knew that mentioning the haircut would be a mistake right now.

One shoulder at a time, Finch slipped off his backpack and propped it against the wall. He squatted to disengage his sleeping bag from the aluminum pack frame.

"Couch is all yours," I said.

"Yeah, okay," he said and sighed, "I'm pretty wiped. Later."

He took his sleeping bag to the living room. I heard the nylon rustle as he unrolled the bag and spread it out. He flopped down on the couch, and the springs squeaked a long time as he tried to find a comfortable position. There was more rustling of nylon, and then silence. By now, I was back in bed.

At one that afternoon, Finch was cooking breakfast. The warm, slightly oily smell of refried beans woke me up. For a second, I thought I was in my mother's house. I hadn't had a bean burrito in a long time. Since I'd moved here, I hadn't even found a place to buy refried beans.

"I couldn't find a good avocado," Finch said, as I walked into the kitchen. "They were all from Florida and I hate those. Smooth-skinned and watery. Half of it is pit, anyhow." He thoughtfully licked the spoon, then stuck it back into the beans and resumed his stirring. "Listen," he said, "I don't mean to get personal, but like, where's David?"

"Didn't Mom tell you? He's gone."

Finch tried to pretend he hadn't expected this. "You guys weren't getting along, or what? Last time I was here everything seemed pretty cool."

"Well," I said, "that was August. I'd only been with David a couple of weeks. Now it's January. We didn't know and understand each other as well as we do now. We both had a spontaneous revelation about our relationship one night. I came home from work and found David in bed with one of the girls in his band. I threw all his possessions out the window, and he left with the girl. We came to the profound understanding that we never wanted to see each other again."

Finch had finished folding the tortillas around the beans and melted cheese. He put the burritos on plates, and then he studied me for a few moments. I both dreaded and looked forward to his inevitable next comment. "You're really skinny, Lucy. You lose all this weight because of David?"

"What do you mean? I'm always thin." I don't usually admit it,
but I can be a real martyr. "Yeah, I guess that's why. The first
week after he left, I barfed every day. Every time I thought about
moving all the way here to live with that turd, it made me sick. I
lost ten pounds. Now, two weeks later, here I am eating refried
beans for breakfast. Progress."

"Bummer."

"Really."

We finished our meal in silence. Finch stared at his hiking
boots. Out of habit, he reached back to adjust his pony-tail. As
his fingers closed on thin air, he blushed. I began to pick the
leaves off a dying plant. Finch lit a Winston. He got up from his
chair, went to the radiator, and sat down on it. He discovered it
was on, and returned to his chair.

"I was doing really good," he said, "but I blew it. Crashed
and burned. I didn't think it would happen this time, but it did.
It's so different from a normal high school, and I've really
learned a lot. But like, I guess I couldn't hack the responsibility. See, they have this honor code. You all agree not to smoke pot
while you go to school there. That way, I guess they figure it will
keep us all more together. We'll be a unit, like, so people won't
end up in cliques and stuff. I hadn't toked since I went up there.
Swear to God. This one day, this guy and me, we decided it would be
fun to do some smoke and walk in the snow. This other guy saw us,
only we didn't know it. Two weeks later, he stands up in Friday
Night Meeting and reports it to the whole school. Man, I'd practically forgotten about it; it wasn't even that fun. Like, I know I
deserved it, but I felt so humiliated.

"I am such a fool. At Granger High, I smoked because I hated
that stinking hole. I smoked and never went to school. Survival.
The only way. But now, at Vermont Outlook, it's different. It's
the school I wanted to go to. You live and work within the community. Like, we're trying to help the locals stop a nuclear power
plant from being built. And I have this really cool girlfriend,
Joanne. She's twenty, and she's really smart, and she's teaching
me marine biology. I was even thinking of taking the SAT's and trying to get into some college. But I blew it.

"They all voted that the two of us that smoked should go away
from the school for awhile and think about whether we wanted to
come back and renew our commitment. After the meeting, Joanne came
over to my room. She told me she was really disappointed in me. I
don't blame her. I've worked hard since September to be close with
everyone at school. And honest. It really meant a lot to me to be
responsible for once. The whole thing is, like, you have to give as

well as take. I guess that's obvious and corny. But we all taught
each other and learned from each other. I know it sounds hippie-
ish, but we really are like a family. Now I've disappointed everyone. I could never face any of them again. You should have seen the
way they looked at me. Like I killed everything for them. In a way,
I've destroyed a lot of what we all worked for. This is not the
first time I've done this, you know."

I knew. We'd been through all this before. Finch had always
had school problems. Even when things were going well, he seemed
to almost deliberately get into trouble. The problem was simply
that he didn't like school. I was tempted to tell him that his situation wasn't as grave as it seemed, and that his friends were being
melodramatic. I was also tempted to remind him that this was his
third high school and there were only a few months left. Couldn't
he have lived harmoniously with his "family" until June? On the
other hand, in our discussion of David, Finch had kindly refrained
from pointing out that in the last three years, I'd had as many "serious" boyfriends as he'd had high schools. I could have told him
that this incident at school would blow over; he could have told me
that I was better off without David. But neither of us would have
felt better and we knew it. To Finch, his banishment was devastating. Once I grasped the enormity of the situation from Finch's
point of view, I couldn't think of anything significant to say.

"What happened to your hair?" I asked.

"What do you think? I'm hiding it? I got it cut. After all this
stuff happened, I was on the bus coming down here. I thought, 'I
have nothing going for me. I'm just a big jerk.' I tried to think of
just one good thing about myself. All I could come up with was my
hair. I had to wait in Boston three hours for the next bus. I was
walking around, and I saw this barber shop that was open. It was ten
o'clock at night. Seemed like an omen to me. The barber's name was
Wesley. He had a little name plaque on his mirror. Straightest guy
I ever saw. He cut it. Took about three minutes. He called me Red. I
was tempted not to tip him for that, but I didn't want anything else
on my conscience. First time I've been in a barber shop since I used
to go with Dad. It still stunk."

Finch stayed with me for five days. I took some time off work.
On the second day of Finch's visit, he told me he was going to stay
in the city. He said he liked it much better than the woods in Vermont. He was going to move in with me and find work as a carpenter. I
didn't say anything. We saw some movies and ate in a lot of restaurants. Finch found a black derby in perfect condition in an antique clothing store. He took me to a blues club that a boy at
school had told him about. I was surprised that Finch knew quite a
lot about blues. It is always hard for me to understand that Finch

can know things that I don't. I can remember teaching him to swim underwater. But I forget about the several years that have passed since we both lived in our mother's house.

By the fourth day, Finch wanted to call his friends at school. He talked for a long time to several people. He used some words and phrases that I had never heard. After the phone call, Finch lost the guilty, uncertain look that had hung over him since his arrival. The next morning when I woke up, Finch was stuffing his clothes into his pack. He had written a two-page apology to his classmates. He would read it the next night at Friday Night Meeting. Everyone would forgive him.

Interactions

- In the first and second drafts, the narrator says on the phone, "When you get here, knock loud. I'm going back to bed." In the third draft, this becomes:

  "Oh. Okay. But when you get here, knock loud, in case I fall asleep again."

  I took the extra pillow off my bed and put it at one end of the couch. It was a long ride from Vermont to the city, and I figured Finch had been awake for most of it. Sheets and blankets were unnecessary, as my brother always travelled with a sleeping bag. I sat down in the kitchen on a straight-back chair to keep from falling asleep, but I fell asleep anyway. Finch knocked so loud, I jumped.

  What impact do these changes have on you? Do they alter your impression of the narrator at all? In what way?
- In the first draft, the narrator says that the smell of the food reminded her of "cozier times and places." In the second draft, she says it reminded her of "a more secure, easier time." In the third draft she says, "The warm, slightly oily smell of refried beans woke me up. For a second, I though I was in my mother's house." How would you characterize these changes? What effect do they have on you as a reader?
- How have your impressions of the story changed from the first draft to the final draft?
- Write a final draft of your character sketch of Finch. Compare your first draft with your final draft. How has your perception of Finch changed? Compare your final draft with those of your group members. Did all of you see Finch in the same way? Did all of you use the same information about Finch in your character sketches?
- Write your own version of a story containing two characters. After writing a first draft, share it with your writing group. Ask group members to write a character sketch of one of the characters in your story. Then compare the sketches with your draft. Have you discovered any-

thing in this process that would enable you to write-and-revise further? Now write another draft.

□   □   □

William Atwill, a professional writer, used the process of selecting, ordering, questioning, and changing when he wrote an article on
athletics for a newspaper. In an early draft, his first two paragraphs
focus on a personal experience.

    If I had to reduce my own participation in athletics to one
memory, it would be an early morning workout one calm spring morning in a eight-oared racing shell. There was no wind and a light fog
obscured the shoreline so that the world was reduced to us--eight
oarsmen and a coxswain sliding silently across the mirrored surface of the St. Lucie River. A cadence quietly tapped out against
the hull brought us smoothly through each stroke in such unison
that each dip of the oars left 3 perfectly spaced swirls of expanding ripples along the smooth wake that trailed behind us. That
morning we could have rowed forever. We were in total synchroniza-
tion, the boat was set, it "ran out" without the slightest hesi-
tancy, and as exhausted as we were we couldn't stop grinning. We
were "on" that day and though no one would ever know it but us, it
didn't matter. Something had blended that morning into the perfect mixture of intellect, teamwork, and mutual admiration.
    The feeling I got that day was that this was what athletics
should be, a celebration, an affirmation of the combined physical
and mental potential that exists within all of us. For this reason, to see athletics only as competition is to misunderstand the
role of sports and to lead to the sort of corruption of thought that
makes both the staging and the boycotting of the Olympics inappropriate national politics. What is necessary to understand here is
the role sports should play in our lives. We must see athletics in
perspective--what it ought to be rather than what it has become.
Particularly this is important within our educational system.

□   □   □

In an intermediate draft, he changed the focus slightly:

□   □   □

    All of us cleared our oars in clean precision, feathered and
slid quietly forward for the next stroke, catching it perfectly

with the coxswain's cadence. Behind us, the swirling "puddles"
our blades left on the mirrored surface of the river ran in two perfectly spaced lines until they disappeared in the fog. This morning everyone felt the magic; all eight of us were rowing together
in such harmony that the long thin racing shell seemed to glide under a power beyond the effort we put into pulling the oars. No one
spoke and no one wanted to quit. So long as the magic of that glid-
ing synchronicity could be maintained we would keep rowing, knowing all the while that no coach, no spectators, and no opposing
crew would ever appreciate this moment of near perfection; this
sense of something shared.

If it were somehow necessary for me to reduce all my memories
of sports to the one that was the most indelible, I think I might
have to choose this experience over all my competitive experiences, and easily over any achievement I witnessed as a spectator.
I learned something about athletics and teamwork that usually is
bankrupted by cliches or misplaced emphasis on winning. I learned
that mind, body, and surroundings can merge in such a way that past
and future vanish and the present moment expands in near-mystic
harmony.

Interactions

- How has the writer reordered his material in the second draft? Underline any new material that was added to the second draft. Go back to
  the first draft and underline any material that has been omitted from
  the second draft. Speculate about why the writer might have made the
  changes he did.
- How do you expect the essay to develop? What do you think the emphasis will be?

□ □ □

In the final version, published in the *Star News,* Wilmington,
North Carolina, Atwill has made new choices:

Athletics in Perspective

William D. Atwill

All of us cleared our oars in clean precision, feathered and slid
quietly forward for the next stroke, catching it exactly with the coxswain's cadence. The swirling "puddles" our blades left on the glassy
surface of the river ran out behind us in two perfectly spaced lines until they disappeared in the mist. This morning everyone felt the mag-

ic—eight of us rowing together in such harmony that the long, thin racing shell seemed to glide over the water effortlessly—and no one spoke or dared ease up. The grace and beauty, the spell of that flowing synchronism, held up to us the mirror of our own potential, but the real significance of this moment was that it occurred one morning in practice, with no coach, no spectators and no opposing crew to define it in the usual context of competition. It was a moment of celebration—athletics in perspective.

These affirmations of the combined physical and mental potential existing within all of us are so often overshadowed by an emphasis on winning and losing that it is necessary to look at what the role of athletics ought to be in our lives rather than what it has become. This is particularly true with regard to the distinction made between athletic programs and physical education in our schools.

Until recently, our athletic programs were only marginally responsive to the needs of the students they were designed to serve. Physical education was largely ignored other than as some compulsory activity during junior and senior high school. And even here, more emphasis was placed on being "dressed out" than on participating in any meaningful learning process.

School sports were the true focus of athletics, and they had become specialized expensive outlets for an elite segment. Those few who were physiologically adapted to be good at football, basketball or baseball had at their fingertips elaborate sports complexes and coaching, while the majority of students were left to confine their sports careers to being spectators. The casualties from this distortion of priorities were the small, the overweight, the awkward and the introverted: precisely those students who had the most to gain from the improved self-image that athletics can provide. Women also suffered; the thought that a woman might actually be interested in participatory athletics was so foreign as to be almost laughable. Competition was, apparently, only of interest to men.

The result of sports programs that culled all but the well-adapted few was that those not chosen lived vicariously through the successes of their school teams and abandoned their own athletic needs.

Much of this misplaced emphasis has changed over the last 15 years with the emergence of progressive academic degree programs offered by departments of Health, Physical Education and Recreation (HPER) at many universities. Now specialists with the knowledge that institutional programs must be broad-based and beneficial to the greatest number of participants are carrying this quiet revolution into the public school system. With reinforcement and encouragement in the home, the ideals of athletics might regain the prominence they deserve, altering entirely this society's perception of sport.

What then are these ideals? Essentially, they hinge on the belief that physical education and athletic programs should be so designed that they actively encourage participation by as many people as possible. These activities should be varied and involve people of all body types and all levels of ability, emphasizing above all else the sense of personal enrichment that flows from living in harmony with one's physical self. In no way should these activities discriminate by sex. The equal access to resources for women should be so logical and well-established that it would not even need stressing here, but the misconceptions regarding women and athletics are so ingrained that it has taken federal legislation to even begin to bring about parity.

Whether an activity is considered an individual pursuit or a team sport, it is the personal satisfaction of playing well that is rewarding. Emphatically, this is not self-indulgent gratification, but the logical consequence of discipline, concentration and hours of practice. What truths are learned about the benefits of this sort of discipline may reinforce other aspects of life. For this reason, athletic programs that instill a positive attitude toward physical activity should be a part of the basic educational opportunity of all children. The chance to participate in structured athletic programs that promote a lifetime of fitness should be as readily available as nutrition programs, since both share the same objectives. Viewed properly, athletics become more than mere fitness, just as physical health is more than simply the absence of disease.

What grows logically out of these ideals is a generation with a lifetime commitment to vigorous physical activity. Community recreation facilities, as well as school programs, become responsive to the real needs of the people they serve, and the shifting fortunes of a few competitive teams become less important than the individual participation of so many former spectators now caught up in their own pursuits of excellence.

Where this view of athletics in perspective leads, hopefully, is to a time when something as momentous as the Olympics can take place in the pure spirit in which it was conceived. Gone will be concern for how many gold medals have been collected by any one country, replaced by an admiration for all the athletes who have come together to truly celebrate the infinite potential of the human body.

Interactions

- In what ways did the article develop as you expected it to? Did anything in it surprise you?
- Compare paragraph one of Atwill's intermediate draft with paragraph one of the published version. What words did he decide to change? What changes has he made in sentence structure? What effect do

these changes have on you as a reader? Why do you think he made these changes?

- Write your own version of the meaning (or lack of meaning) of sports in your life. Keep a record in your journal of how you handled the initial and subsequent drafts of the piece.

□ □ □

Writing-and-Revising Three

(a) Look at several drafts of a paper you have written. What changes have you made? What strategies could you now use to make new choices?

Revise the paper using whatever writing-and-revising strategies you choose. Share the paper with your writing group and ask them to speculate about why you made the changes you did. Then share your writing-and-revising process with your group, explaining why and how you revised the piece into its present form.

(b) Select two incidents that you feel have had a great impact on your life. Write a one-page sketch of each. Read these drafts to your writing group and ask them to help you decide which one to develop further.

Write a second draft of the sketch you chose. Experiment with some of the strategies you have discovered in this chapter.

What writing-and-revising strategies did you decide to use in order to write the second draft? What did you discover by doing so? What strategies would you use to write another draft?

Now bring your paper into final form.

(c) Write an autobiographical account of some period in your life. (It may be a few days, a few months, or a few years—the important thing is to impose a set of time limits.)

Use appropriate writing-and-revising strategies to re-envision your paper.

(d) Write a story about seeing someone you haven't seen for a while (a friend, a member of your family). What changes do you notice in him or her? In yourself? Can you explain why?

Write another draft. And a third if the second draft doesn't get you where you want to go.

(e) Think of some early childhood memories. Write a short paragraph about each. Share these vignettes with your writing group and ask them to help you choose one for further development.

Now write a draft of a longer piece.

(f) Write a biographical sketch about someone you know (a family member, a friend, a neighbor). In other words, tell a story about your subject. Then put the paper aside, and write down every aspect of your subject you can think of: character traits, personality, physical appearance, interests, mannerisms, age, family background. Now compare your list with the draft of your story. What changes would you now make in what you have written, in order to present your subject more fully.

Write another draft of the story.

(g) Select a figure in a field that interests you (such as art, literature, biology, sociology, history, music, political science, whatever). Research that person's life and choose one period to explore in a short biographical sketch. Write a draft and share it with your writing group. Ask members of your group if there is more information they would like to know.

Write another draft, using whatever writing-and-revising strategies seem useful.

Awaiting the poetic mews

Chapter 4

The Writer's Journal/Notebook/Diary

A journal is a record of experiences and growth, not a preserve of things well done or said. I am occasionally reminded of a statement which I have made in conversation and immediately forgotten, which would read much better than what I put in my journal. It is a ripe, dry fruit of long-past experience which falls from me easily, without giving pain or pleasure. The charm of the journal must consist in a certain greenness, though freshness, and not in maturity.

HENRY DAVID THOREAU

Writers write about their perceptions of the world. At the start, they may simply record images, ideas, impressions, or intuitions, just in order to remember them and think about them. This recording might take the form of journal or diary entries, or notes on cards or in notebooks, and it may be in whole sentences and paragraphs or just fragments, parts of sentences or even single words. The point is that writing about their experience helps them understand it.

Writers write even when they don't think they have anything to say because they trust that their writing will help them discover meanings that they didn't realize were there. The following entry from Virginia Woolf's diary is a good example of how a writer began with "nothing to say" and discovered something meaningful:

Friday 29 January
Shall I say "nothing happened today" as we used to do in our diaries, when they were beginning to die? It wouldn't be true. The day is rather like a leafless tree: there are all sorts of colours in it, if you look closely. But the outline is bare enough. We worked: after lunch we walked down to the river, to that great mediaeval building which juts out into the river—It is I think a vast mill. And we came back early, so that L. might have tea be-

fore he went to a Committee at Hampstead. After that I bought our food, & did not observe much of interest. But the fact of the day for me has been a vague kind of discomfort, caused by the eccentric character of the new servant Maud. When one speaks to her, she stops dead & looks at the ceiling. She bursts into the room 'just to see if you are there'. She is an angular woman of about 40, who never stays long in any place. I believe she lives in dread of something. She puts down plates with a start. Mrs. Le Grys says that she herself is going mad, with Maud's peculiarities. She has just announced that she is the daughter of a Colonel. I am sure her brain if full of illusions, poor creature; & I shouldn't be surprised at anything. The only question is, how she contrives to exist.

The Diary of Virginia Woolf (1915)

After asking whether she should say that "nothing happened today," Woolf catches herself and says, "it wouldn't be true." And she goes on to talk about how important it is to look closely for colors in even a "leafless tree." She then gives a few details of her daily life before hitting on the really significant moment or thought of that day: observing her new servant. The amount of description compressed in just a few sentences of her entry gives us a vivid picture of Maud, making us want to find out much more about her. So Woolf has managed to make what to her might have been a rather mundane day seem interesting. To her, the "great mediaeval building" is rather ordinary, but for those of us who don't live in rural England, this building seems unusual, even mysterious.

Parts of Woolf's entry are private—only she or someone who knows much about her life would know who "L." is. Other parts any reader can understand. Actually, she was writing for herself. Her point in recording events from her life was to gather material for her novels as well as to preserve fragments of her daily life for further reflection. Probably, too, she kept her diary as a record of self-discovery, for as Graham Greene says, "Writing is a form of therapy ... sometimes I wonder how all those who do not write, compose, or paint can manage to escape the madness, the melancholia, the panic fear which is inherent in the human situation."

Like Woolf, most writers keep records of their experiences, so that they can retrieve not only memories of the events themselves but also their impressions of those events at the time they happened. For example, Rico Simonini, a student writer, described in his journal an experience he had while visiting his family in Italy:

Mt. Vesuvio towered ominously in the background. Towering some 3,000 feet, she was a reminder of her subjects' vulnerability

as she overlooks Pompeii--a victim of her wrath some 2,000 years
ago. I gazed at her from the roof top for a while, then turned and
looked out into the bay--pale blue--serene. In the distance I was
able to distinguish the faint outline of Capri--some ten miles
out. I looked over the expanse of the town in wonderment. Many of
the buildings were of white stucco and stone--dating back to the
turn of the century. Torre del Greco lay before me--untouched, unscathed by what some call progress.

The people still thought the way their ancestors did--still
lead a way of life as prescribed by their parents. Here, traditions were still strong--as strong and dominating as the volcano
which towered over them. They were children of Vesuvius--and like
the mountain, they'd never change.

My cousin gave me a tap on the shoulders--it was time to
leave. As much as I knew I had to, I was reluctant to. I couldn't
leave the hometown--a haven from the cold, cruel modern world. I
couldn't part with my relatives. I felt I was doing them an injustice by staying a mere 24 hours.

I went downstairs and looked at them--tears already forming
in their eyes more quickly than they were forming in mine. I wanted
to just forget everything and stay--but Rome awaited me as did the
jumbo jet that would take me back to the crime and turmoil of New
York. I was a Brooklyn boy now--I had to remember that, though the
moment made it extremely difficult to do so.

I found it extremely difficult to reconcile myself as we were
saying last words to each other. I heard the sound of an automobile
horn--that was my ride. Never before, it seemed, did I hear a noise
so displeasing and painful as that horn. Time grew short, I said to
myself--feeling as if Death himself was summoning me with his
knell. I walked up to my aunt and embraced her. As I kissed her on
the cheek, a feeling of tremendous guilt overcame me. Then, reluctantly we let go. I picked up my bag and walked to the door. In the
archway, I turned and faced them--my aunt was wiping the tears
from her eyes. As a means to console myself, I promised them that
I'd return.

Then again forcing my every step, I said "Ciao," and made my
painful exit, saying to myself, "I shall return."

Interactions

- What do you think Rico had in mind to do in this journal entry? Was
he just "jotting down" impressions? How do you know?
- On the strength of this entry alone, what questions might you want to
ask Rico about his brief portrait of Torre del Greco? What more, if
anything, would you like to know?

- How "private" is this entry? Is Rico writing only for himself? What more do you need to know to have these reflections mean to you what they obviously mean to Rico?
- Write an explanation of what you feel to be the difference, if any, between private and public writing.
- If Rico were a member of your writing group, what writing-and-revising strategies would you suggest for him to bring his journal entry into a final piece of writing?

□   □   □

Rico's actual experience of saying goodbye to his relatives was just a brief moment, yet he managed to say a great deal about it. Later, he decided that this entry showed promise as a sketch for a longer piece which could explain how life is very different in Italy than in the United States. He began reformulating his impressions by adding some specific examples to the second paragraph:

The people still thought as their ancestors did. They still
lead a way of life as prescribed by their parents. I looked down
upon a busy street and watched the cars pull to the side to allow
the passage of an old man in his horse-driven cart. I glanced
across at a terrace and noticed an old woman sitting in a rocker
with children about her listening attentively. By the movements
of her hands I knew she was telling a story--and a good one at that.
Here, traditions were still strong--as strong and dominating as
the volcano which towered over them. They were children of Vesu-
vio--and like the mountain--they'd never change.

Rico realized after rereading his draft that he must bridge the gap between what he knew of the events and what the reader needed to know in order to understand them. In other words, he realized that he had to do things for other readers that he didn't have to do for himself in his journal.

Interactions

- In the final version of Rico's essay, which follows, note in the margin any material he has added. Speculate about why he chose to add the material he did.

□   □   □

ARRIVEDERCI NAPOLI

Rico Simonini

Mount Vesuvio towered ominously in the background. Towering
some three thousand feet, she reminded her subjects of their vul-

nerability as she overlooked Pompeii, a victim of her wrath some
two thousand years ago. I gazed at her from atop the roof of Zia
Teresa's old stucco building, then turned and looked out into the
bay--pale, blue, serene. In the distance, Capri was but a faint
outline some ten miles out. I looked over the expanse of the town in
wonderment. Many of the buildings, like my aunt's, were of white
stucco and stone--dating back to the turn of the century. Torre
del Greco lay before me. A small town just south of Naples, she had
survived the massive earthquake which rocked the countryside and
now she was there; untouched, unscathed, by what some call progress.

Strange that I should find myself here during my semester
break from N.Y.U. I had been appointed an N.Y.U. Scholar on the basis of my achievements and as a result I found myself taking part in
the Scholars' "Venture to Rome" trip. It was as if Destiny herself
wanted me in Italy this week. I had managed to slip down to Naples
while the rest of the Scholars went to Florence. I was told that was
a poor trade-off (Naples for Florence) but I felt this was much
more important to me. The trip had come at just the right time. I
felt the sudden need to get away when the semester had ended. There
had been tensions everywhere--at home, in school, and with a very
special friend. I had felt alone--perhaps even rejected. I needed
the change in atmosphere. Naples was a tremendous bonus. It would
offer me the opportunity to go back in time to trace my past and the
people in it. In going back I would be able to face that which lay
ahead. I needed answers to many questions. Torre del Greco, the
hometown, was where I'd try to find them.

La bella Torre was a haven from the rest of the world. The people still thought as their ancestors did. There was a tremendous
sense of morals and the Catholic Church. I looked down upon a busy
street and watched the cars pull to the side to allow the passage of
an old man in his horse-driven cart. Across the street on an opposite terrace was an old woman sitting in a rocker with children
about her listening attentively. By the movements of her hands, I
knew she was telling a story--and a good one at that. I wondered how
many cars would pull over to let an old man get by in Manhattan or
how many elderly people in the City had such a young attentive audience. Here, traditions were still strong, as strong and as dominating as the volcano which towered over them. They were children
of the Vesuvio--and like the mountain--they'd never change. The
people still carried out their lives as people did in my grand-
mother's times. The old were held in highest respect. People re-
spected each other. Cemeteries were still crowded with people
who'd pay their daily respects. Though most of the people weren't
extremely wealthy, they were content with the lives they led. Ev-

eryone took everything "nice and slow"; no rush to get anywhere because the people knew they'd always get there.

I stood there, on the rooftop, for a while, then focused again at the majestic structure of Mount Vesuvio, thinking of its awesomeness and power. Then I thought: the family; there is no greater force, no greater structure in all of Torre del Greco, Naples, or all of Italy than the family. "It's a shame," I thought, "how this precious tradition and part of life was so warped and shattered in America." Even those who came from here and went to the States were somewhat tarnished by what they may attribute to the "American air." It was here, though it was only a day, where I experienced the tremendous love, honor, and respect that existed with "the Family." Here more than anywhere else I had realized the predominance of these forces. Nothing, it seemed--not money, not power, not even death--could stand between the binding forces that held the "Family" together.

Alas, I felt fortunate that I was able to experience this first hand. It was that something which I felt was lacking when I had left. It was the answer that I'd hoped to find. It was this feeling that I had to take back with me and try to reinstate. It was that feeling of the sense of the "family" that I had experienced in Torre del Greco where it was still unadulterated, uncorrupted-- pure.

My eyes wandered about. I looked at the cemetery where I had paid my respects to Grandpa just a few hours ago. Further inland was my uncle's motorcycle shop where I could only stay an hour because of my scarcity of time. Then, further uphill was Zia Maria's house. I had just left her in a very painful goodbye. I remember her watering eyes as she forced a smile in wishing me farewell. I remember embracing her and not wanting to let go and the way I saw her waving from the terrace while wiping the tears from her eyes with a lace kerchief she had embroidered herself. God, why couldn't time have stopped for a month or so. This was not enough time--but perhaps having it was enough. The entire day had been draining--both physically and emotionally. I thought it would end when I left Zia Maria, but before leaving I was taken to visit my great aunt. I had never seen her before but upon meeting her, I felt I had known her for ages. After seeing me she said that she felt she could die happy now that she had seen me. This was too much for me. Here I was on her rooftop trying to collect my thoughts as I looked upon this isolated town protected by the shadow of the mountain.

My cousin tapped me on the shoulders; it was time to go. I went downstairs to bid farewell to Zia Teresa. I looked at her swollen tearing eyes behind those horn-rimmed, thick glasses. Her tired

old grey hair was ruffled, tied in a bun as an attempt to improve
its appearance. I saw tears track down her wrinkled face as we
hugged. After I kissed her on both cheeks she let go reluctantly.
She spoke to me in the language that I had learned before English,
the language of the hometown, Torre del Greco. "My house is always
open to you," she had said. I couldn't help but feel a tremendous
feeling of guilt overcome me. I wanted to forget about everything
and stay, but Rome awaited me as did the jumbo jet that would take
me back to the dirt, grime, and turmoil of New York City. I couldn't
reconcile myself as we said last words to each other. I looked at
her, an eighty-five year old woman, and wanted to cry, but my
masculinity prevented me from doing so. I was in turmoil--I could
go.

    In the midst of this strife, I heard the sound of an
automobile horn--that was my ride. Never before, it seemed, did I
hear a noise so displeasing and painful as that horn. Time grew
short, I said to myself, as if Death himself was summoning me with
his knell. Without falling apart, I picked up my bags, bid a final
farewell and walked towards the door. Something inside me wanted
to put the bags down and embrace her again as I stood in the
archway. I controlled this--I was a man now. I knew I'd be back and
promised them so. I said, "Ciao!" and made my painful exit. As we
drove away I thought of the time I spent here and though very brief
(a mere twenty-four hours) I shall value it along with what I've
learned more than all the riches there are to go for on earth.

Interactions

- What do you find out in the final version that you didn't know in the
  journal entry?
- What has Rico added to his final version that suggests he's writing for
  a reader rather than for himself?
- Write an account of a trip you have taken recently, whether it be for a
  short distance—a subway or bus ride, for example—or a long one—
  such as a journey to another city, town, or country.
- Write about an experience you have had with "going home." Then
  read your first draft to your writing group and ask them to tell you
  what you need to develop further in order to make your experience accessible to a public audience. Write another draft.

☐   ☐   ☐

    Nathaniel Hawthorne, a nineteenth-century American novelist,
also kept a journal of his impressions and experiences. One entry
talked about an experience he had while out walking one night.

    Mr. Leach and I took a walk by moonlight, last evening, on
the road that leads over the mountain. Remote from houses, far

up on the hill-side, we found a lime-kiln, burning near the road-side; and, approaching it, a watcher started from the ground, where he had been lying at his length. There are several of these lime-kilns in this vicinity; they are built circular, with stones, like a round tower, eighteen or twenty feet high; having a hillock heaped around in a considerable portion of their circumference, so that the marble may be brought and thrown in by cart-loads at the top. At the bottom there is a doorway, large enough to admit a man in a stooping posture. Thus an edifice of great solidity is composed, which will endure for centuries, unless needless pains are taken to tear it down. There is one on the hill-side, close to the village, wherein weeds grow at the bottom, and grass and shrubs too are rooted in the interstices of the stones, and its low doorway has a dungeon-like aspect, and we look down from the top as into a roofless tower. It apparently has not been used for many years, and the lime and weatherstained fragments of marble are scattered about.

But in the one we saw last night a hard-wood fire was burning merrily beneath the superincumbent marble—the kiln being heaped full; and shortly after we came, the man (a dark, black-bearded figure, in shirt-sleeves) opened the iron door, though the chinks of which the fire was gleaming, and thrust in huge logs of wood, and stirred the immense coals with a long pole; and showed us the glowing limestone—the lower layer of it. The glow of the fire was powerful, at the distance of several yards from the open door. He talked very sociably with us, being doubtless glad to have two visitors to vary his solitary night-watch; for it would not do for him to get asleep, since the fire should be refreshed as often as every twenty minutes. We ascended the hillock to the top of the kiln; and the marble was red-hot, and burning with a bluish, lambent flame, quivering up, sometimes nearly a yard high, and resembling the flame of anthracite coal, only, the marble being in larger fragments, the flame was higher. The kiln was perhaps six or eight feet across. Four hundred bushels of marble were then in a state of combustion. The expense of converting this quantity into lime is about fifty dollars, and it sells for 25 cts. per bushel at the kiln. We talked with the man about whether he would run across the top of the intensely burning kiln for a thousand dollars barefooted; and he said he would for ten; he said that the lime had been burning forty-eight hours, and would be finished in thirty-six more, and cooled sufficiently to handle in twelve more. He liked the business of watching it better by night than day; because the days were often hot, but such a beautiful night as the last was just right. . . . Here a poet might make verses with moonlight in them, and a gleam of fierce

fire-light flickering through them. It is a shame to use this bril-
liant, white, almost transparent marble in this way. A man said
of it, the other day, that into some pieces of it, when polished, one
could see a considerable distance; and instanced a certain grave-
stone.

The Heart of Hawthorne's Journals (1838)

□   □   □

Hawthorne took the sketch about the lime-kiln from his journal
and developed it into a short story, "Ethan Brand." What follows is
the opening of that story:

Ethan Brand

Nathaniel Hawthorne

Bartram the lime-burner, a rough, heavy-looking man, begrimed
with charcoal, sat watching his kiln at nightfall, while his little son
played at building houses with the scattered fragments of marble,
when, on the hill-side below them, they heard a roar of laughter, not
mirthful, but slow, and even solemn, like a wind shaking the boughs of
the forest.

"Father, what is that?" asked the little boy, leaving his play, and
pressing betwixt his father's knees.

"Oh, some drunken man, I suppose," answered the lime-burner;
"some merry fellow from the bar-room in the village, who dared not
laugh loud enough within doors lest he should blow the roof of the
house off. So here he is, shaking his jolly sides at the foot of Graylock."

"But, father," said the child, more sensitive than the obtuse, middle-aged clown, "he does not laugh like a man that is glad. So the noise
frightens me!"

"Don't be a fool, child!" cried his father, gruffly. "You will never
make a man, I do believe; there is too much of your mother in you. I
have known the rustling of a leaf to startle you. Hark! Here comes the
merry fellow now. You shall see that there is no harm in him."

Bartram and his little son, while they were talking thus, sat
watching the same lime-kiln that had been the scene of Ethan Brand's
solitary and meditative life, before he began his search for the Unpar-
donable Sin. Many years, as we have seen, had now elapsed, since that
portentous night when the IDEA was first developed. The kiln, however, on the mountain-side, stood unimpaired, and was in nothing
changed since he had thrown his dark thoughts into the intense glow
of its furnace, and melted them, as it were, into the one thought that
took possession of his life. It was a rude, round, tower-like structure
about twenty feet high, heavily built of rough stones, and with a hill-

ock of earth heaped about the larger part of its circumference; so that the blocks and fragments of marble might be drawn by cart-loads, and thrown in at the top. There was an opening at the bottom of the tower, like an oven-mouth, but large enough to admit a man in a stooping posture, and provided with a massive iron door. With the smoke and jets of flame issuing from the chinks and crevices of this door, which seemed to give admittance into the hill-side, it resembled nothing so much as the private entrance to the infernal regions, which the shepherds of the Delectable Mountains were accustomed to show to pilgrims.

There are many such lime-kilns in that tract of country, for the purpose of burning the white marble which composes a large part of the substance of the hills. Some of them, built years ago, and long deserted, with weeds growing in the vacant round of the interior, which is open to the sky, and grass and wild-flowers rooting themselves into the chinks of the stones, look already like relics of antiquity, and may yet be overspread with the lichens of centuries to come. Others, where the lime-burner still feeds his daily and night-long fire, afford points of interest to the wanderer among the hills, who seats himself on a log of wood or a fragment of marble, to hold a chat with the solitary man. It is a lonesome, and, when the character is inclined to thought, may be an intensely thoughtful occupation; as it proved in the case of Ethan Brand, who had mused to such strange purpose, in days gone by, while the fire in this very kiln was burning.

Interactions

- Compare Hawthorne's journal entry with the opening of his story. What do you find in the journal entry that appears in the story? What are the differences between the journal entry and the story? Is the journal entry private? In what sense? How would you know from reading the journal entry that it was an account of personal experience rather than the opening of a short story?
- Write your own version of a particular evening. Then dramatize that private journal entry by reformulating it into a story.
- Go to the library and read portions of the published journals of several writers. (Henry David Thoreau, Anaïs Nin, and Leo Tolstoy are a few of the many writers whose journals have been published.) Write a paper in which you discuss the value, as you perceive it, of keeping journals, based on your research and your own experience.

☐   ☐   ☐

The journal entries of Rico Simonini and Nathaniel Hawthorne presented here are long and detailed, but often writers just jot down some idea that seems important at the time, even if they don't know why. For example, over a period of nine years, Hawthorne wrote three separate journal entries that eventually took shape as *The Scarlet Letter:*

> To show the effect of gratified revenge. As an instance, merely, suppose a woman sues her lover for breach of promise, and gets the money by instalments, through a long series of years. At last, when the miserable victim were utterly trodden down, the triumpher would have become a very devil of evil passions—they having overgrown his whole nature; so that a far greater evil would have come upon himself than on his victim.
>
> (1836)

> Insincerity in a man's own heart must make all his enjoyments, all that concerns him, unreal; so that his whole life must seem like a merely dramatic representation. And this would be the case, even though he were surrounded by true-hearted relatives and friends.
>
> (1837)

> To represent a man in the midst of all sorts of cares and annoyances—with impossibilities to perform—and almost driven distracted by his inadequacy. Then quietly comes Death, and releases him from all his troubles; and at his last gasp, he smiles, and congratulates himself on escaping so easily.
>
> The life of a woman, who, by the old colony law, was condemned always to wear the letter A, sewed on her garment, in token of her having committed adultery.
>
> (1844)

□   □   □

Like Hawthorne, Franz Kafka, a twentieth-century Austrian-Czech writer, kept a journal in which he wrote down various ideas for stories. But Kafka, like many other writers, couldn't always tell immediately what would work and what wouldn't. Thus, his diaries are full of false starts, aborted stories, beginnings that never end, snatches of dialogue, characters who never develop. For example, he began this entry that initially appeared to him to be going somewhere:

> The river stretched calmly between the meadows and fields to the distant hills. There was still sunshine only on the slope of the opposite shore. The last clouds were drifting out of the clear evening sky.
>
> *The Diaries of Franz Kafka* (1912)

But then, in the same diary entry, he reevaluated what he had just written:

Nothing, nothing. . . . For a moment I thought I saw something real in the description of the landscape.

Of course, many of Kafka's diary entries did eventually develop into published stories just like Hawthorne's. And that's what makes the dead-ends and dry runs so important—writers never know what will work before they try it.

□   □   □

Another American novelist, Henry James, used his notebooks in a slightly different way. Concerned with how he would actually develop a particular piece, James carried on a dialogue with himself about his writing. In one entry, he recorded a story told to him and immediately began to speculate about how he could develop that story into a piece of fiction:

De Vere Gardens, W., November 12th, 1892.

—Two days ago, at dinner at James Bryce's, Mrs. Ashton, Mrs. Bryce's sister, mentioned to me a situation that she had known of, of which it immediately struck me that something might be made in a tale. A child (boy or girl would do, but I see a girl, which would make it different from *The Pupil*) was *divided* by its parents in consequence of their being divorced. The court, for some reason, didn't, as it might have done, give the child exclusively to either parent, but decreed that it was to spend its time equally with each—that is alternately. Each parent married again, and the child went to them a month, or three months, about—finding with the one a new mother and with the other a new father. Might not something be done with the idea of an odd and particular relation springing up 1st between the child and each of these new parents, 2d between one of the new parents and the other—through the child—over and on account of and by means of the child? Suppose the real parents die, etc.—then the new parents marry each other in order to take care of it, etc. The basis of almost any story, any development would be, that the child should prefer the new husband and the new wife to the old; that is that these latter should (from the moment they have ceased to *quarrel* about it) become indifferent to it, whereas the others have become interested and attached, finally passionately so. Best of all perhaps would be to make the child a fresh bone of contention, a fresh source of dramatic situations, *du vivant* of the original parents. *Their* indifference throws the new parents,

through a common sympathy, together. Thence a 'flirtation,' a
love affair between them which produces suspicion, jealousy, a
fresh separation, etc.—with the innocent child in the midst.

The Notebooks of Henry James

A year later, James was still turning the story over in his mind,
as this notebook entry reveals:

August 26th, 1893 (34 De Vere Gdns.).

I am putting my hand to the idea of the little story on the
subject of the *partagé* child—of the divorced parents—as to
which I have already made a note here. The little *donnée* will
yield most, I think—most *ironic* effect, and this is the sort of
thing mainly to try for in it—if I make the old parents, the original parents, *live,* not die, and transmit the little girl to the persons they each have married *en secondes noces.* This at least is
what I ask myself. May I not combine the ironic and the *other*
interest (the 'touch of tenderness'—or sweetness—or sympathy
or poetry—or whatever the needed thing is), by a conception of
this sort; viz.: that Hurter and his former wife each marry again
and cease to care for the child—as I have originally posited—as
soon as they have her no longer to quarrel about? The new husband and the new wife then take the interest in her, and meet on
this common ground. The Hurters quarrel with *them* over this,
and they separate: I mean each of the Hurters separate afresh.
Make *Hurter* die? His 1st wife survives and becomes extremely
jealous of his 2d. I must remember that if Hurter dies, the situation breaks, for his wife then gets the whole care of Maisie; which
won't do. No, they both live.

Three months later, James wrote out a detailed plan in his notebook for how the plot of *What Maisie Knew* would develop in eight to
ten chapters. But as he soon discovered, he needed far more than his
eight to ten chapters to develop his story, and the final version grew to
thirty-one. Meanwhile, he had many problems to work out, and he
solved them by writing in his notebooks. After writing the first half of
his novel, he thought he saw clearly the way to proceed:

The Vicarage, Rye, September 22d, 1896.

I've brought my little history of 'Maisie' to the point at
which I ought to be able to go on very straight with it;. . . .

But he then reached another impasse: how to get everyone off-
stage at the end of the novel so that Maisie finally could decide for
herself what she would do about the miserable situation of being used

as a pawn between two sets of parents. Again, James solved the problem in his notebook by deciding to use a scenic method (that is, techniques of the stage):

December 21st, 34 De Vere Gdns., W. (1896)

I realise—none too soon—that the *scenic* method is my absolute, my imperative, my *only salvation. The march of an action* is the thing for me to, more and more, *attach* myself to: it is the only thing that really, for *me*, at least will *produire* L'OEUVRE, and L'OEUVRE is, before God, what I'm going in for. Well, the scenic scheme is the only one that I can trust, with my tendencies, to stick to the march of action. How reading Ibsen's splendid *John Gabriel* a day or two ago (in proof) brought that, FINALLY AND FOREVER, home to me! I must now, I fully recognize, have a splendid recourse to it to see me out of the wood, at all, of this interminable little *Maisie; 10,000 more words* of which I have still to do. They can be magnificent in movement if I resolutely and triumphantly take this course with them, and *only if I do so.*

In the space of some thirty pages of entries in his notebooks, written over a span of some five years, James formulated and reformulated his initial idea. The opening of *What Maisie Knew,* published in 1897, presents that idea in its final form:

What Maisie Knew

Henry James

The litigation had seemed interminable and had in fact been complicated; but by the decision on the appeal the judgment of the divorce-court was confirmed as to the assignment of the child. The father, who, though bespattered from head to foot, had made good his case, was, in pursuance of this triumph, appointed to keep her: it was not so much that the mother's character had been more absolutely damaged as that the brilliancy of a lady's complexion (and this lady's, in court, was immensely remarked) might be more regarded as showing the spots. Attached, however, to the second pronouncement was a condition that detracted, for Beale Farange, from its sweetness—an order that he should refund to his late wife the twenty-six hundred pounds put down by her, as it was called, some three years before, in the interest of the child's maintenance and precisely on a proved understanding that he would take no proceedings: a sum of which he had had the adminstration and of which he could render not the least account. The obligation thus attributed to her adversary was no small balm to Ida's resentment; it drew a part of the sting from her defeat and compelled Mr. Farange perceptibly to lower his crest. He was unable to produce the money or to raise it in any way; so that after a squabble scarcely less public and scarcely more decent than the original shock of battle his only issue from his predicament was a compromise proposed by his legal advisers and finally accepted by hers.

His debt was by this arrangement remitted to him and the little girl disposed of in a manner worthy of the judgment seat of Solomon. She was divided in two and the portions tossed impartially to the disputants. They would take her, in rotation, for six months at a time; she would spend half the year with each. This was odd justice in the eyes of those who still blinked in the fierce light projected from the tribunal—a light in which neither parent figured in the least as a happy example to youth and innocence. What was to have been expected on the evidence was the nomination, *in loco parentis,* of some proper third person, some respectable or at least some presentable friend. Apparently, however, the circle of the Faranges had been scanned in vain for any such ornament; so that the only solution finally meeting all the difficulties was, save that of sending Maisie to a Home, the partition of the tutelary office in the manner I have mentioned. There were more reasons for her parents to agree to it than there had ever been for them to agree to anything; and they now prepared with her help to enjoy the distinction that waits upon vulgarity sufficiently attested. Their rupture had resounded, and after being perfectly insignificant together they would be decidedly striking apart. Had they not produced an impression that warranted people in looking for appeals in the newspapers for the rescue of the little one—reverberation, amid a vociferous public, of the idea that some movement should be started or some benevolent person should come forward? A good lady came indeed a step or two: she was distantly related to Mrs. Farange, to whom she proposed that, having children and nurseries wound up and going, she should be allowed to take home the bone of contention and, by working it into her system, relieve at least one of the parents. This would make every time, for Maisie, after her inevitable six months with Beale, much more of a change.

Interactions

- What new information is presented in the opening of *What Maisie Knew* that you didn't know from reading James's notebook entries?
- Write a short essay in which you trace the development of *What Maisie Knew* from the journal entries to final form.
- In your own journal, work out your plans for a piece you're writing.

☐ ☐ ☐

Writers can do other things with their records besides solving problems with a particular idea as James did or experimenting with various approaches to a story like Kafka. Sometimes, a writer can analyze a journal entry, using it as a point of departure for a larger piece of writing. Paula Carmichael, a student writer, chose to use this strategy with three related entries from her journal:

```
one:   All glows, muted pink
       and hums, low and vibrant

two:   The sum
           force
               meaning
         truth
       presence      energy
           total
       one
         all     all
                   one
           strive
               be
       make
           beginning
                       end

three:

-------------------------------words-------------------------
------------------------- phrases ---------------------------
---------------------------------------float----------------
------------------------------- i know----------------------
---------------------------------------------ecstasy-----
```

Paula then wrote an essay in which she interprets what these brief, fragmentary entries meant to her:

OF VISIONS AND REALITY

Paula G. Carmichael

In September of 1978 I moved to my aunt's home in San Diego. Before this my life had followed a path that had been chosen for me: grade school, junior high, high school . . . going straight into college was the logical thing to do. Most people could not understand why I decided to go to work instead. The only guide I had was a strong feeling that this was what I ought to do and by the time I was hired as a parking lot attendant I was beginning to doubt this. The transitory nature of my life confronted me everywhere: I was in a new place, living, working, and moving among strangers. The few people I worked with were known as "Joe from Lot 24" or "Hernando the lunch relief guy" and the like. To someone who has grown up in a relatively small town the feeling of going days or months without talking to close friends or even seeing an old acquaintance is profoundly unsettling. Even the surroundings were strange: the houses stacked one on another contrasted sharply with the old house with half-acre yard I'd grown up in, the palm trees and cacti made me yearn for the thick foilage of the New York region, and most noticeably, the panoramic view of mountains was utterly alien to my myopic suburban eyes. However, it would be untrue to say that these things made me feel only insecurity and home-sickness; they also charged me with a desire to take hold of this new situation, my new life, and truly make it my own. My everything's-a-drag-and-there's-nothing-I-can-do-about-it-so-let's-go-get-stoned attitude was quickly fading . . . I wanted to learn Everything, about people, life, the meaning of it all . . . then I would be happy.

My journal entries of this time deal with these feelings in great detail. What strikes me now is the sense of urgency about them--I wanted to unravel the secrets of the universe RIGHT THEN; I wanted assurance that I was doing the RIGHT THING. Underneath the urgency lies fear--fear that things would not work out, that I would be crushed by the weight of the world and never know why.

One night, not long after I'd arrived there, I awoke from a dream feeling at once exquisitely calm yet exhilarated. My mind surged, reeled, and fell back, awed and contented. Then I wrote the following, which I have copied from my journal.

one: All glows, muted pink
        and hums, low and vibrant

two: The sum
      force
        meaning
   truth
  presence   energy
    total
  one
   all   all
        one
    strive
      be

```
        make
            beginning
                        end

three:

-----------------------------words-----------------------
------------------------ phrases -------------------------
------------------------------------float----------------
------------------------------ i know--------------------
-----------------------------------------ecstasy-----
```

The first entry describes what was in the dream: a presence all around and within. The "me" is purposely omitted for there was no singular entity "I"--whether I was this presence or it was I, I can't tell, for no boundary existed between us.

The next entry tries to describe the nature of this presence as a sum of all things. Thinking of this revelation of totality, feeling it now as I did then, a sense of wonder at everything fills me. Simply to exist is the greatest miracle I could ask for.

The last thing I saw in the dream before I awoke were phrases that floated: reading them, I knew why things existed, what I was to do in life, everything. I awoke, seeing the shapes of those words, unable to recall what they said. I panicked--I had to know them; I could not let them slip away, for I would be lost and confused again. Suddenly I was calmed . . . somehow I knew the words themselves weren't important for their meaning was etched forever in some part of my mind.

After this experience I always felt a sureness about what I chose to do and things that happened to me. When I returned to New York after two years in San Diego, my viola teacher said, "It is so good to see you--you are becoming a 'mensch'--a real, full person!" She was right; I had stopped worrying about what I was supposed to be doing and had instead learned much from both good times and bad. I have become more honest with myself about my good and bad points and, knowing these, am learning to turn both to my advantage and, hopefully, the advancement of humankind.

Interactions

- What made these particular journal entries significant for Paula?
- Find an entry—or a series of entries—in your own journal to reflect on the way Paula did? Write a draft. Then share your draft with your writing group and explain how you used your journal.

Writing-and-Revising Four

(a) Select an entry from your journal that could be developed further or that could be used as a point of departure. Then write a draft of an essay.

Read your essay to your writing group. Ask the group to help you determine if any parts of your essay need clarification for a public audience. (In other words, is anything in your essay still too much like a private journal entry?) Now rewrite your essay.

(b) Experiment with writing about the sorts of things the writers in this chapter felt were worth recording. Use their journal entries as starting points for your own. You may also want to use your journal as a "commonplace" book—writing down interesting things that you read in other classes or on your own.

(c) Using a journal entry as a point of departure, write a paper that develops a personal experience into a story. First read the journal entry to your writing group and see how their suggestions change your own impressions of what you had originally written.

While you're writing this paper, make notes to yourself in your journal describing what you intend to achieve and how the paper is changing as you're writing it.

Read the draft to your writing group and explain how it moved from private journal entry to public writing. Ask the group to indicate where they would like to see further development (for example, perhaps some of your language is still too private); then write another draft.

(d) Use your journal to experiment with new ways of writing. Some examples of writing experiments you could do include:

Description of an everyday object: a paper coffee cup, for example, a room, a building, a street—anything that forces you to pay attention to fine detail

Dialogues with a friend, an antagonist, a younger self, an inanimate object, a historical figure

Dream transcription

Monologues, screenplays, TV scripts

Earliest childhood memories, significant moments in the past, happy moments, sad ones

Character studies

Stories from your family

Stream of consciousness, free-writing

Letters

Conflicts with people, with situations

How someone else sees you, or how you would like to be seen
Fantasy, science fiction
A moment five years from now (What will you be doing?)
A moment five years ago (Where were you?)
Poetry
Reactions to events in the news, perceptions about the world,
  reflections on the quality of life

(e) As you're working on a writing project, perhaps in another
course, keep a writing-and-revising journal in which you describe
how you feel about what you're doing, how you see your writing,
what sorts of frustrations and breakthroughs occur. Be as specific as you can about each choice you make in any piece you're
working on. Write down changes that you make and your motives for making them.

(f) Go to the library and find a published journal/notebook/diary to
investigate further. Write a paper in which you define the character and purpose of the journal you've read. In writing this paper, you may want to refer to studies of journal writing or
specific sources about the writer of the journal you've chosen.

    In bringing this piece of writing into final form, try to give
some indication about what you perceive as being the journal-
writing process of the person whose journal you are analyzing.

(g) Choose a published journal/notebook/diary of a novelist, poet,
journalist, philosopher, politician, painter, or other figure.
(Among the available published journals are those by Ralph Wal-
do Emerson, F. Scott Fitzgerald, Paul Gauguin, Alice James,
Carl Jung, Mark Twain, Dorothy Wordsworth.) Also examine
some of what your chosen journal writer has actually produced
as finished work, trying to find passages from the private journal
that correspond to the public final product—like the excerpts
from the journals of Hawthorne and James in this chapter.
(Many published journals are edited or indexed to show corre-
spondences with the author's finished work.)

    Write a paper in which you discuss how the finished work
developed from writing in a journal.

Chapter 5

Writing-as-Discovery

I write entirely to find out what I'm thinking, what I'm looking at, what I see and what it means. What I want and what I fear.

JOAN DIDION

Writers seldom know exactly where their ideas are going until they begin to write. They commit themselves temporarily to one direction to see where it will lead. If it goes nowhere, or if they don't like where they're going, they try another starting point. You, too, will have to take an idea and see where it will go before you know for sure whether it suits your purpose. You might find in the middle of a paper where you're going to end up or where you might actually be starting from. In other words, as you write-and-revise, you make discoveries about what you want to say and how you want to say it. Writing-as-discovery—that process of finding out what you want to say, of realizing what you didn't know you knew—is something that every writer experiences.

Writing-as-discovery spans the entire process of writing, combining both finding something to say and figuring out how to say it. Professional writers, conscious of their strategies in writing, have said explicitly that they rely on this process of discovery. E. M. Forster, for example, once said, "How do I know what I think until I see what I say?" John Updike has said that "writing and rewriting are a constant search for what one is saying," and Adrienne Rich has said of her poetry that "poems are like dreams; you put into them what you don't know you know."

Although the process of discovery is inherent in the act of writing, you can deliberately set out to discover something, using writing as a probe, a means of exploring a territory. This conscious exploration helps you get started and keep going, helps you find material and make connections, allows you to solve potential problems and construct a tentative order. You do this probing in order to generate possibilities, to create options out of the chaos of your preliminary ideas. Various devices enable you to discover possibilities in this deliberate way—for example, creating a list of your ideas or making a preliminary outline of your thoughts. The point in listing and outlining is not to follow absolutely your initial selection and ordering; rather, it's to begin a search, to begin the process of making meaning. Robert Brown, a professional writer who is also a psychologist, even constructs elaborate maps of his territory, one of which looks like the one on page 78.

Brown begins by placing the general idea of his paper—in this case, "moral and ethical responsibilities"—in the middle of his page. He then generates as many ideas as possible, suspending his questioning and ordering by scribbling thoughts randomly all over the page. Finally, he draws lines and arrows to connect one thought to another. His map thus allows him to see many possibilities—many ideas and how they might connect with each other—before he begins the actual placing of one idea after the next sequentially down the page.

Conscious discovery techniques are a powerful resource because they postpone temporarily the final structuring of a piece of writing. These techniques force you to seek out the many possibilities available so that your final selecting and ordering of material will be your strongest choice. The purpose of these techniques, then, is simply to proliferate possibilities, to discover options, to help you begin writing and keep writing, until you discover what you want to say and how to say it. In a sense, these techniques keep you from committing yourself to a connected batch of sentences before you're really ready to commit yourself; you generate a lot of raw material before you start shaping it.

In this chapter you'll explore in detail the usefulness of two discovery techniques, ones that student writers have found helpful in formulating and reformulating their ideas. One discovery technique is free-writing; the other is changing perspective.

Free-writing is simply writing nonstop for a predetermined length of time—three minutes, five minutes, ten minutes, whatever. The critical factor is to keep writing—that is, without pausing to edit, to cross out a word, to correct spelling, to think about what to write next, even to reread what you've written. You keep writing so that you can get something down on paper and start your mind working. The point is to explore every idea that comes to mind without judging prematurely whether or not it's important or unimportant. Free-writing provides you not only with material to write about (your selecting process) but also with connections between one idea and the next.

Eric Hoffert, a student writer, used free-writing to explore the theme of humor, a subject he felt he didn't know very much about. But by writing, he found out that he did indeed have something to say:

Paradigms determine truths
METATHEORETICAL

Scientists have 2 responsibilities: 1. and 2. To
LUNDEEN: Scientist has 2 responsibilities.
Carl: seek out truth.
1. To ...
2. present apart from observer

Data do not exist and cannot be proven
Evolution

Theories should be devices to fit data
not vice versa   Sherlock Holmes
LEVONTIN·SCIENCES
Racist doctrine — Agony March April 76

Data as well as theories are subject to
revisions: "Are blacks lower than whites in intelligence"
Incumbent upon scientists
to rise up and object when other
scientists violate these
responsibilities

Characteristics of science
Accepts Casually
Is empirical
Is interested in reality
Is public
Is amoral
Is a method
Is uncertain

Scientists should accept:
universal ones

VERSUS
DOGMA

Technologists Interaction the other
one feeds the other
Scientists

Moral and
Ethical Responsibilities

Scientists risk loss of credibility
↑ in turn to mystical
RECTIFICATION OF SCIENCE

We can know only within limits of tolerance
BRONSKI

Lucoievicz

(Technology)
Application of
knowledge

Buckley
World made people ...
Earthlings
(knowledge)

Bronowski may be
Science but process
amoral are
scientists are human
conducting are human
and they are ...

Most responsibility informed
What is more offer those
scientists have offer those
decisions than ...

What is funny? Here I am, almost finished with the first term
of Expository Writing, and I still don't know the definition of
humor. I don't know what humor is but I continue to laugh my head
off at certain things. I mean I really <u>sweated</u> it out with trying to
figure out what humor is and what its sources are. But my wrestling
continues.

Let's see. What's funny? I thought <u>Animal House</u> was funny. I
thought <u>Airplane</u> was funny. I especially think the new issue of
the <u>Plague</u> (NYU student magazine) is very funny. Here's an item
which I thought was hilarious. I mean, hilarious, as in I was
laughing so hard, I was crying. OK, let's analyze as we go along. (I
haven't thought this out!) First off, look at the writing of "God-
awful Falafel." When I first saw this writing, I thought it was Arabic. I mean, it looks Arabic. But then I saw what it said and I
laughed out loud. Why? Because it was funny. Is that a good reason?
Isn't that why we usually laugh? OK, we've established something.
We laugh because something is funny. What's funny about it? Whenever I ask myself what humor is, I always come to this realization:
It's funny because it's true. Well, this doesn't make sense. I
mean, is it funny when I say $E=mc^2$? No . . . No. . . . When I spoke
of laughter, I defined it as a kind of release, like crying. I said
that laughter was a release of built up anxiety and tension. . . .
(For example, in the cartoon depicting John Anderson's fantasy
about being President we laugh at our own high expectation for
ourselves when we have failed. We are empathizing. I guess.)
Shoot! All I've done here is come back to my original ideas. Darn
it! Well at least I fully understand why I laugh at this funny cartoon of John Anderson. I once wanted to be President too, you know.

Interactions

- If Eric were a member of your writing group, what strategies would
  you suggest to him in order to develop further the ideas in his free-
  writing?

□   □   □

It's very easy to read through this passage of free-writing and locate where Eric discovers something: "OK, let's analyze as we go
along"; "OK, we've established something"; "Well this doesn't make
sense." Eric is actually having a discussion with himself on paper by
asking himself questions and attempting to answer them: "I mean, is
it funny when I say '$E=mc^2$?' No." By asking yourself questions and
answering them in writing, you can begin exploring ideas that may
find their way into your papers. Free-writing allows you to try ideas
out, to take risks, to experiment with a new approach. If you get into

the habit of exploring ideas in writing, you will discover what you want to say and have your ideas in much clearer focus when you get down to writing your "first" drafts of whatever you want to write.

Interactions

• Quickly list three topics you might want to write about.

Free-write (that is, write nonstop without letting your pen leave the paper) for three minutes on each topic. Time yourself or have a friend watch the clock.

Read back over what you have written. Locate one idea from each of the three free-writings. Put each idea on the top of a blank sheet of paper.

Free-write for another three minutes about each idea.

What have you discovered about your three topics?

• Read your free-writings to your writing group. Which topic do they feel would be the most interesting to develop further? Which topic do you feel holds the most promise?

• Save your free-writing. You may want to develop it into an extended piece of writing later on.

Eric used free-writing as a way of generating ideas for a paper he was assigned to write to fulfill the following assignment.

□　□　□

Analyze Kurt Vonnegut, Jr.'s "Harrison Bergeron" and Woody Allen's "A Brief Yet Helpful Guide to Civil Disobedience." In a short essay, distinguish, if possible, between the characteristics of an essay and a story. Is one expository and the other creative? Consider the following questions: What relationship do you see between them? What is your response to them? How do they differ? How can you answer those questions in such a way that your response is personal rather than canned, alive rather than anesthetized.

The following is Eric's free-writing:

My response to these two pieces of writing would certainly be "canned" if the assignment were not so "creative." When one answers questions such as "What relationships do you see between them?", "What is your response to them?" and "How do they differ?" the initial reaction is "I will now turn into a computer." I'd love to say "phooey!" to the approach but it is not easy to break with tradition. How are we taught to write? Basically, an analytical, step-by-step approach. An Introductory Paragraph. The Body of the paper consisting of an ordered arrangement of thoughts. A Concluding Paragraph. In my wildest dreams, a paper is written with a digression on world events at the beginning, a conclusion in the middle and an introductory paragraph a little bit after the conclusion but before the outline which is written backwards. To get a proper outlook on writing an "essay" I should put my thoughts on a moebius strip.

Eric decided to write an essay using his "wildest dreams" as a point of departure. The following is the result:

MY WILDEST DREAMS

Eric Hoffert

Therefore, I conclude the following: the two essays are concise and alive. Each piece has a distinct, original voice. Each piece is trying to relay a message. Woody Allen infers the absurdity of revolution; the silliness of oppressor vs. oppressed. In a somewhat more circumventious manner, Vonnegut infers the idea that there is something wrong with how people judge each other; all men were created equal?

If all men were created equal, everybody would write the same essay, everybody would have the same style and say the same things. Sometimes I wonder. . . .

When one answers questions such as "What relationships do you see between them?" and "What is your response to them?" and "How do they differ?" the initial reaction is "I will now execute this in a manner similar to that of a computer. I will analyze. I will take the argument step by step using one idea per paragraph. I will write an outline. I will execute. I will turn on. I will turn off." I'd love to say phooey to the standard approach, but it is not so easy to break with tradition. Writing essays in the "academic style" is a trait that has been stamped and ingrained into us since we first wrote about Abraham Lincoln. Is this good? Is this right? Just look at how we are taught to write. Basically, using a step by step approach. An introductory paragraph. The body of the paper, consisting of ideas built up into paragraphs (organized previously using the traditional outline). A concluding paragraph. In some of my more whirled reveries, I think of a different paper. I'd start with my thoughts, whatever they were; be it lust or be it food or be it graphs of ellipsi. Thus my mind would be started on its new travels down the crooked street. How about the conclusion next? An introductory statement in the middle but a little bit after the outline which is written in reverse order and in hieroglyphics. To

get a proper outlook on writing this, I might even put my ideas on a
moebius strip. Something. We should take risks. Take them, you
know.

But taking risks does not include anaesthetic writing. If I
may say so, I suffer from it as much as the next guy. Not only has
the "academic style" been stuffed into our heads, but so has the
idea of "What does she want?" This attitude is also manifested as
"What does he want?" or "What does it want?" "It" referring to some
slimy 3 headed monster. Even as I write this, I realize that in some
ways, I am writing for "What she wants." But luckily this happens
to coincide with what I want. And that's important. You must pursue your ideas, go with your instincts. Next time you write an essay, think of a nice purple moebius strip floating on your
synapses. Tell Harbrace to take a walk.

In this essay, I will attempt to analyze two pieces of writing. These pieces of writing are "Harrison Bergeron" and "A Brief
Yet Helpful Guide to Civil Disobedience," by Kurt Vonnegut Jr.,
and Woody Allen, respectively. I will discuss the relationships I
see between the two writings. I will then discuss the effectiveness of each paper. After I have done this, I will show why there is
truth to my opinion.

Interactions

- Compare Eric's free-writing with paragraph three of his essay. What
  similarities do you notice? What discoveries did Eric make in his
  draft?
- How does Eric respond to the assignment asked of him? What, if anything, surprised you about his approach to the assignment?
- Eric was spoofing a particular academic writing style. Write your own
  parody of any writing style or piece of writing you choose—for example, a bureaucratic message, a poem by a particular author. After
  writing a first draft, ask your writing group to tell you what they
  think you're parodying and then show them the original (if there is
  one).

□   □   □

By free-writing, Eric discovered both the main ideas for his essay
and a way of ordering them. Then, by writing an expanded draft of
these ideas, he discovered still more things to say. All writing involves
this process of discovery, but free-writing is a device for starting this
process by generating as many initial options as possible.

A second discovery technique that writers use in order to in-
crease their options and continue their writing is the procedure of

changing perspective, of looking at what they have written from a different vantage point.

Blas Royo, a student writer, used this strategy when he was writing a story about a Saturday night drag race. The first time he told the story, he told it from the perspective of the driver of one of the cars.

FULL SPEED BACKWARDS

Blas Royo

It was Saturday night which, to the kids, translated as racing night. Racing fever had again struck Broward County in Upstate New York, as it does every year, sooner or later. Every young guy who owned a sports car took part in the races held each weekend at Bluff's Creek, on the outskirts of town. Naturally I, enjoying cars as I do, was no exception.

I myself was the owner of a brand new 1980 Trans Am. It was a shiny white color, with a black firebird engraved on the hood that covered a four hundred forty cubic inch power house engine. It had halogen headlamps that were hidden within the slanted front end of the car. It was beautiful, as well as fast (it did 85 mph cruising). For this reason I had accumulated easy victories weekend after weekend. I was now the top driver of the county in street racing. Since there was little competition for me, I decided to escape tonight from racing and go to the movies with my girl Cindy.

I was in my house getting dressed as quickly as possible so I could arrive early at Cindy's house. I put on a pair of Sasson jeans and western boots to go along with a bright orange pullover. I looked in the mirror at myself for a minute and gave myself a smiling approval. Then I gave myself a quick application of Brut "for men," and was off to the garage.

In the garage, I unlocked the car door and climbed in. I inserted the ignition key and turned the car. Suddenly the power-plant under the hood let loose in a thunderous roar. I got out of the car and removed the glass panels of the T-roof. I stored them in the rear of the garage and climbed back in the car.

All I needed now was some music. I pulled out from under the seat the new wave/rock group Cars' latest tape and inserted it in the tape player. The music shot out of the quadraphonic speakers in the rear. Now with the loud music blasting, I was ready to go. I pulled out of the driveway, made a left, and roared down the street quickly drowning the music from the radio.

I arrived at Cindy's house and parked. I looked for her, but she wasn't around, so I turned the car off. Then I sat calmly in the car waiting for her. I took notice of her house which struck me as extremely impressive. It had a two car garage and a great big green lawn in front. Her house represented to me the model home of suburbia U.S.A.

Fifteen minutes had elapsed when I heard a sound at the front door of Cindy's house. Finally Cindy appeared. I must admit she looked gorgeous. I walked to the porch to greet her.

Me: Hi, Cindy. You look absolutely adorable.

Cindy: Thanks. Are you trying to sweet-talk me?

Me: No. C'mon the car is waiting.

We reached the car where I let her, and then myself, in. I started up the car, shifted gears and pulled out.

I was headed for the expressway to the Big Apple when I drove up by the railroad tracks at the end of town, where I was caught by a red traffic light.

Cindy began to apply the last touches of makeup to her face. To me she looked divine, but then girls are never satisfied with the way they look.

In the distance I heard loud music and hysterical laughter. The sounds seemed to be growing louder, so much so that I could hear some of the lyrics to the song on their radio. They went something like this:

"It isn't true about cocaine,
that it makes you numb, as well as insane,
and if you don't believe me, give it a try,
but don't sniff too hard or your brain might fry"

Suddenly the car appeared in my rear view mirror. It came up and aligned itself with my car. It was a very old brown Chevrolet Impala that squeaked like a mouse and shook like a blender. I looked in their car and could only see the driver. He was slim and had a ghostly complexion. He possessed an intellectual look to him, like he belonged behind a microscope studying cancerous tissues. The other passengers, which I couldn't see, were probably on the floor drunk on half a can of beer. The driver had his eyes firmly fixed on Cindy. The poor devil probably never came close to seeing a girl as pretty as Cindy. He was practically salivating. I accelerated the car to warn him that he best look elsewhere or he would end up racing me.

But to my surprise he accelerated his car right back. I couldn't believe it. He had actually challenged me to a race in his jalopy. Did he know of my racing reputation in Broward County? I was going to "show him who's boss," or at least that is what I thought.

We waited for the traffic light to turn green. Cindy was still applying make up to herself and was not aware of the race that was about to take place.

The traffic light turned red . . . yellow . . . GREEN! We shifted gears and pressed the pedal to the floor. In the sudden acceleration, Cindy's eyeliner went flying into her nostril. Then, to my surprise, I saw the brown jalopy speeding away from me, faster than I could imagine. What went wrong? Something felt strange. I hit the brakes, and came screeching to a halt. I checked the gear box and went into a state of shock. I had accidently shifted the car into REVERSE!

Suddenly Cindy came alive, yelling . . .

Cindy: Are you nuts? Taking off like that. You made me jam my eyeliner right into my nostril!

Me: (chuckling) I'm really sorry Cindy.

Cindy: Yeah sure. Just take me home. You've blown it, buster.

Me: But Cindy . . .

Cindy: "But Cindy" nothing. Let's go, and I mean it.

So I took her home as she wished. My racing days are over now. The following day after that embarrassing incident I sold my brand new Trans Am. But believe me, the problem is far from over, I still get nightmares of losing races to intellectual looking drivers. . . .

Interactions

- List the events of the story as they happened. How does the narrator's perspective influence the way we see the events?
- List all the facts you know about the narrator. Then write a character sketch of him.
- If Blas were a member of your writing group, what suggestions for revision would you make?
- Write a news account of what actually happened in the story. Compare your summary with those of other members of your class.

□　□　□

In order to see other possibilities for his story, Blas decided to rewrite the piece from a different vantage point, this time from the perspective of a passenger in the second car.

Please, don't misunderstand me. I'm not saying that I don't enjoy living in Upstate New York, it's just that it's tough living in a town where the favorite sport is chess! I mean how would you feel living in a town where the kids are only allowed to go to Discos when Saturday night mass is canceled? Yes, well, now you can

begin to understand how boring living in a place like this can be,
and why the kids here try most anything to get a little excitement.

It was a hot Saturday afternoon in June. Fred, Rich, and me
were (like always) hanging around the high school chewing the fat.
"There's got to be something we can do other than sit around like
rocks all day," said Fred. "You're right Fred, why don't we all decide on something we can do together," I said. We all sat around
silently in deep thought when suddenly Rich burst out extremely
excited, "I know, I know." 'What, What?" I asked. Richard turned
to me and said, "It's not for sure yet, but I may be able to get my
old man's car." "Really?" Fred asked joyfully. "Yeah, wait here,
I'll go ask," said Rich. Fred and me watched Rich start running
home and kept our fingers crossed that all would turn out well.

After some twenty-five minutes had elapsed, Rich rounded the
corner and pulled up in front of the school. Rich shut off the motor
and climbed out. "Well, are you guys ready to go cruise?" asked
Rich. I was still staring at the car in disbelief. It was a brown
Chevrolet Impala about 10 years old (even though it looked like
20), with four bald tires and a hanging muffler. "Oh my God," said
Fred. "You can say that again," I said. "Oh my God," Fred repeated.
Rich looked at us both a bit angrily and said, "Hey I never said it
was a Mercedes." Well anyway, we climbed in the car (after cleaning the dust from the seats) and left for a hopefully exciting
ride.

Main Street was busy on Saturdays. As we rode by Fred whistled
at every girl visible, and by mistake, even at a transvestite.
Richard was busy steering the car, whose power steering probably
stopped working a couple of years ago. I myself kept quiet in the
back seat, though I suspect the Budweiser probably had something
to do with me being so quiet.

It started getting late and Rich decided he should take the
car back home, but first he wanted to take one last drive around
town. We passed by the town hall, and then by a Burger King to pick
up a bite to eat before starting back home.

We were on our way back when a red traffic light stopped us
right by the railroad tracks. A gleaming white Trans Am came roar-
ing up next to us, where it now stood perfectly aligned with Richard's Impala. We looked over into the car where there sat a
gorgeous blonde with clear blue eyes and cherry red lips. "Who is
that knockout?" asked Fred. "Listen, if I knew who she was I'd be
with her and not with you." I said. "What do you think of her Rich?"
I asked. But Richard didn't respond. He was hypnotized, and practically salivating. The savage next to the blonde girl in the
Trans Am looked like the captain of the University of Notre Dame

football squad. The gorilla looked over at our car annoyed with
the way Richard kept looking at the blonde. "Hey Rich, cool it man,
look somewhere else. I think that savage with the blonde is going
to pulverize you if you keep staring at his girl," I said to him.
But Richard was in his own world, nothing could penetrate his concentration. The gorilla in the car gave Richard a warning by roar-
ing his engine. At that very moment the blonde gave Rich a smile,
and Richard then roared his motor right back! "Oh no!" said Rich.
"Rich are you nuts? You just challenged that animal to a race!"
said Fred. Richard's eyes opened wide, and began growing pale.
"Hey guys, I think I'm gonna faint," said Rich. "Oh no you don't.
You got into this mess, now stick it out Rich," said Fred.

The light turned yellow. Both drivers gave each other a quick
look, and then faced the traffic light once again. GREEN! The
light changed and both drivers shifted and pressed hard on the gas
pedals. Instantly blue smoke rose from the spinning wheels of the
Trans Am. In our car Rich stepped hard on the gas and sent his
glasses flying from his nose. "Oh, no, I can't see a thing!" yelled
Rich. "What?" asked Fred. "My glasses," said Rich. Then suddenly
out from the back seat I yelled, "Rich straighten the wheel you're
heading for a wall!" Fred was reaching for Rich's glasses on the
floor when I noticed that the Trans Am was nowhere in sight. "Hold
it. We won," I yelled. Richard hit the brakes hard and Fred's head
slammed into the radio--which then changed stations. The Trans Am
was about 200 feet behind us. "The jerk must have shifted into reverse!" said Rich proud of his victory. We all were laughing, that
is until I checked the street where Richard's muffler lay in one
complete piece. "Hey Rich, does this car have a loose muffler?" I
asked. "Yeah, and it's a real pain. Why?" asked Rich. "Well," I
said, "Your troubles are over." "Oh really?" said Rich. "Yes, you
see it's sitting on the starting line," I told him. "Well what do
you know," said Rich, and he backed the car up to where the muffler
lay. He got out of the car, picked it up, and brought it to the car.
"Well guys," he said, "how do you like our first place trophy?"
Fred and I looked at the rusty, old muffler and began to laugh hys-
terically. Rich then climbed into the car, shifted into drive, and
we were on our merry way once again. . . .

Interactions

- How has the sequence of events changed in the second version? What
  do you know now that you didn't know before? Describe the attitude of
  the new narrator toward the events of the story.
- Write a news account of this version of the story. Compare your summary with those of other members of your writing group.

Now compare your account with the one you wrote previously. Do they deal with the same story?

Write another news account in which you attempt to explain both versions of what happened.

- Briefly write your own version of the story, assuming the role of one of the participants or acting as a third-person narrator. After you have completed your draft, write down your answers to the following questions.

1. What new information, if any, did you add to the events of the story?
2. How would you characterize the attitude of your narrator?

Exchange stories with another writer in your class. Answer the same two questions about your classmate's story. How did you as a reader perceive the writer's intentions?

□   □   □

The way Blas chose to change perspective was to tell the story from the vantage point of another character. In expository prose, where there are no characters per se, there's still the perspective of the person relaying the information. In order to change perspective in a way comparable to the way Blas did, a writer would have to look at different sides of an issue. Dianne Ray, for example, wrote a paper about the marijuana controversy:

MARIJUANA DECRIMINALIZATION: YES OR NO?

C. Dianne Ray

Over the past decade there has been continual controversy as to whether or not marijuana is harmful to the human organism. Some quarters see marijuana as relatively harmless and believe that criminal sanctions should be eliminated (decriminalized) for possession of small amounts. Others believe, however, that until conclusive evidence has been gathered to prove that marijuana is not harmful that the criminal sanctions should remain in force.

The anti-decriminalization forces have been encouraged of late by recent reports that claim marijuana is indeed harmful to those who smoke it. At Tulane University, neurophysiologists have studied the effects on the brain of the "most psycho-active cannabinoid, Delta-9 THC, and have concluded that it definitely interferes with the brain's normal functions." It has been observed that even occasional smokers experience "euphoric, muddled thinking, and sequencing, poor planning abilities and

general disorientation as well as poor time and space orientation."[1]

Pro-decriminalization quarters, however, do not view the
new data on the harmful effects of marijuana as conclusive. Prestigious groups such as the American Public Health Assocation,
American Bar Association, National Council of Churches, National
Commission on Marijuana and Drug Abuse and National Education Association have viewed the medical claims and have found that mod-
erate usage of marijuana does not create any serious health
problems.[2] Dr. Lester Grinspoon, Associate Professor of Psychia-
try at Harvard Medical School, states that many of the claims regarding the hazards of marijuana (that it causes insanity, is
crimogenic) have proven baseless and that the new ones are often
based not on clinical evidence, but on experiments or laboratory
analyses that even experts would find difficult to interpret.[3]
Dr. Grinspoon states further that the new data which is available
is, at best, too inconclusive for use as the basis for public policy.[4]

The Consumer Union states that "of course no drug is harmless
to all persons at all dosage levels or under all conditions of
use,"[5] but the belief that criminal sanctions are the proper societal response to the possession of a harmful product or substance
is not consistent with society's usual approach to products, even
harmful ones.[6] CU draws an analogy to alcohol and nicotine, which
have been proven to be harmful substances. These drugs are definitively harmful, yet society has not deemed it necessary to arrest
or imprison those found using them.[7] Keith Stroup, National Director of the National Organization for the Reform of Marijuana
Laws, states that it is indefensible that "otherwise law-abiding
citizens who happen to smoke marijuana are branded as criminals."[8] As CU puts it, "Why should marijuana smokers, unlike alcohol drinkers and tobacco smokers, be deliberately subjected to
damage by society in addition to any harm they may do to themselves
through the use of the drug?"[9]

The controversy about the effects of marijuana seems des-
tined to continue for years to come. Each side believes very firmly that it is correct in its assumptions and believes its way is
best for society as a whole. Until evidence as to the long term effects of marijuana is found, the controversy will continue and the
question of whether marijuana is hazardous or just a recreational
thrill will continue to be asked.

Notes

1. Dr. Richard A. Hawley, "Science, Politics, and Marijuana,"
   America, 22 September 1979, p. 133.

2. Peter Stroup, "Controversy over Policy Controlling
     Marijuana Use : Pros & Cons," Congressional Digest,
     February 1979, p. 44.
3. Lester Grinspoon, "Controversy over Policy Controlling
     Marijuana Use : Pros & Cons," CD, p. 52.
4. Ibid.
5. "Marijuana: The Legal Question," Consumer Reports, April
     1975, p. 265.
6. Ibid.
7. Ibid.
8. Stroup, p. 44.
9. "Marijuana: The Legal Question," p. 265.

Bibliography

Grinspoon, Lester. "Controversy over Policy Controlling
     Marijuana Use : Pros & Cons." Congressional Digest,
     February 1979, p. 52.
_____. Marijuana Reconsidered. Cambridge : Harvard
     University Press, 1971, pp. 362-416.
Hawley, Richard A. "Science, Politics, and Marijuana." America,
     22 September 1979, pp. 133-4.
"Marijuana: The Legal Question." Consumer Reports, April 1975,
     pp. 235-6.
Stroup, Keith. "Controversy over Policy Controlling Marijuana
     Use : Pros & Cons." Congressional Digest, February 1979, pp.
     40, 44, 48.

□ □ □

When Dianne rewrote her essay, she changed perspective:

□ □ □

I am here today to make the point that marijuana smokers are
not the enemy. They span all socio-economic and age groups. They
are your neighbors, your friends, even those you least suspect. If
marijuana is harmful it is not just a criminal problem but a potential health problem.[1] If it is a health problem, treat it as such.
     There is a great amount of misinformation about marijuana.
Much of this misinformation has its origins in the 1930s with the
so-called "educational campaign" of the Federal Bureau of Nar-
cotics. This campaign was based largely on alarming exaggera-
tions and distortions such as marijuana causes insanity and has
crimogenic effects.[2] Today a great deal of the new data is tainted

by this misinformation. Many of the old claims regarding the hazards of marijuana have been proven groundless; and the new ones are not based on scientific clinical evidence but on analyses which are difficult to interpret.[3] The new data (marijuana causes brain damage and fetal malformations), at best, is too inconclusive to be used as the basis or justification for public policy.[4] Many prestigious organizations agree that marijuana does not present any serious health problems as have many studies done by governmental and private special commissions that have studied the marijuana problem.[5]

I do not mean to intimate that marijuana is absolutely harmless. "Of course, no drug is harmless to all persons at all dosage levels or under all conditions of use,"[6] but what should society's response be to drugs or substances, harmful or not? The idea that arrest and imprisonment are the proper societal responses to the possession of a harmful product or substance is not consistent with society's usual approach to products, even harmful ones. Alcohol and tobacco have been proven to be detrimental to human health, yet society has not deemed it necessary to impose sanctions against those found possessing them.[7] Why should marijuana smokers be branded criminals when other harmful drugs are left sanctionless?

A constant tension exists in our society between individual liberties and the need for reasonable societal restraints. It is easy to go too far in either direction, and it is especially true with regard to drugs. Too often individual liberties are submerged in the making of public policy. The state in the case of marijuana must justify its interference with individual liberties or decriminalize marijuana use. The criminalization of marijuana is a destructive, unjustifiable part of public policy.

Notes

1. Peter Stroup, "Controversy over Policy Controlling Marijuana Use: Pros & Cons," Congressional Digest, February 1979, p. 52.
2. Lester Grinspoon, Marijuana Reconsidered. Cambridge: Harvard University Press, 1971), p. 363.
3. Lester Grinspoon, "Controversy over Policy Controlling Marijuana Use: Pros & Cons," Congressional Digest, p. 52.
4. Ibid., p. 54.
5. "Marijuana: The Legal Question," Consumer Reports, April 1975, p. 266.
6. Ibid., p. 265.
7. Ibid.

Bibliography

Grinspoon, Lester, "Controversy over Policy Controlling
     Marijuana Use: Pros & Cons." Congressional Digest,
     February 1979, p. 52.
     _____. Marijuana Reconsidered. Cambridge: Harvard
     University Press, 1971, p. 363.
"Marijuana: The Legal Question." Consumer Reports, April 1975,
     p. 265-66.
Stroup, Peter. "Controversy over Policy Controlling Marijuana
     Use: Pros & Cons." Congressional Digest, February 1979, pp.
     50, 52.

Interactions

- Describe the attitude of the writer toward the subject in the first draft. How does the attitude change in the second draft. Defend your claim by referring to particular sentences which show this change.
- How has the use of source material changed from draft to draft?
- If you were to write a paper on the same subject, what additional information would you like to know? How would you find that information?
- If Dianne were a member of your writing group, what suggestions for writing-and-revising would you make?
- What can a writer learn from changing perspective in the way that Dianne did?
- Based on the information Dianne gave, or what you yourself have found in your research, take a stance for or against the decriminalization of marijuana or any other controversial issue and write a letter to the editor of your local newspaper. Then change perspective and write another letter opposing your original view. Share the letters with your writing group and ask them if they would be convinced by what you said.

□ □ □

Dianne's way of altering perspective was to change from presenting both sides of an issue to arguing in favor of one side. Blas, on the other hand, changed the narrator of his story. A third way to alter perspective in a piece of writing is to make the focus more general or more particular.

Patrick McGrath, a student writer, altered perspective as he wrote-and-revised an essay for which he had designed his own assignment:

Do you think that the major popular art forms (film, music) of today are superior or inferior to the major art forms before the

twentieth century (literature, theater, etc.). Why do you feel
the way you do?

In response to this assignment, Patrick wrote the following first draft,
in which he dealt with popular culture in a general way:

"Everyone will be a star," Andy Warhol said, "for fifteen
minutes." The red eye of the television camera has penetrated into
every crevice of the world, capturing every possible human activity. The concept of the "global village" is as near to realization
as it ever will be. Without even leaving our homes we can go to war
in the Middle East, witness starvation in Africa, or just listen
to anybody from anywhere. Has the destruction of distance or sepa-
rateness diminished our capacity to imagine or experience what
the world is like? It has certainly made imagination unnecessary,
but was it ever? To admit, as I do, that the quality of contemporary
culture is bland (to say the least) is recognizing the obvious.
But to say that culture in America, or anywhere else, was thriving
and vital 100 years ago is ridiculous. The domination of society
by consumerism is the cause for cultural decline, not a drop in the
collective intellect. Art and literature in the past were always
the work of the elite or the aristocracy, a small minority of society. Did a Welsh coal miner in 1850 appreciate Dickens or Jane Aus-
ten any more than an American truck driver in 1980? I think not.

What has changed drastically is the commercialization of society. In previous centuries, the masses were so alienated from
society that they barely recognized their rights economically
and culturally. The rise of the working classes created vast new
markets for selling things. As populations and wealth grew, more
and more could be bought and sold. Art may have once been the private possession of the elite, but as society leveled off, music,
theater, and sculpture were accessible to many.

Shifts in popular culture are always a reflection of consumer
interests, not intellectual taste. What will be produced is not
what is most interesting or provocative, but what will sell. In
the 1950s, when rock music was developing, entirely new genres in
film, theater, fiction, and journalism were developing in pro-
test to the bland cultural institutions of the "establishment."
It is, however, the ultimate irony of post-world war American history that the "counter-culture" and some of the heroes became as
commercialized and prosaic as the institutions they attacked.
"Underground" newspapers, such as the Village Voice or Rolling
Stone, have become multi-million-dollar commercial enterprises
reaching a wide audience, rather than remaining underground papers catering to a small and unprofitable readership.

Artistic standards reflect the values of a society and are
not abstract entities unto themselves. With a decline in quality
as a result, contemporary culture is accessible to an entire society, whereas before the twentieth century, art and culture were
the monopoly of the aristocratic elite while the masses toiled
away in obscurity.

Though popular art today is generally inferior in contemporary culture, that fact is secondary to the crucial realization
that the dissemination and quality of art have more to do with the
economic and commercial realities of society than as a representation of intellectual taste.

Interactions

- Write a piece in which you reflect on what Patrick has said. Do you agree with his point of view? Why or why not?
- Write your own response to Patrick's writing assignment. Read your first draft to your writing group and ask them to suggest ways of changing perspective. Pick one and write another draft.

□   □   □

After rereading his first draft, Patrick had a feeling that he
could strengthen his paper by focusing on one popular artist in particular, rather than attempting to tackle popular culture in general. He
therefore revised his original assignment:

Who is your favorite popular artist? What makes him or her excep-
tional?

BRUCE SPRINGSTEEN: IN THE TRADITION
OF THE BEATLES

Patrick McGrath

The enthusiasm and energy which John Lennon conveyed in his
final interviews leads me to suspect that he would be a little disappointed in those of us who feel his death symbolizes the death of
rock and the idealism of the Beatles. While the loss of John Lennon's life is irrevocable, his work and his message live on: there
is still hope of a better way of life through music. There will be
no better evidence of this continuity than when Bruce Springsteen, the man once heralded as, "the future of rock and roll,"
hits the stage in Madison Square Garden on December 18. In the
years following the Beatles, rock had gone askew; it has taken
Bruce Springsteen to come along and set things straight.

The Beatles represented an artistic and an ideological revolution: rock and roll could be used as a peaceful weapon against war and injustice. The social revolutions of the 1960s were never fully realized; the Beatles broke up and young radicals slinked back into the establishment to become old and cynical. Yet, while the political potency of rock may have been drained, it emerged out of the 1970s, a decade of blandness and apathy, as a vigorous art form in the person of Bruce Springsteen, who not only reconnected with the musical roots of the Beatles, but re-established rock as an artistic force capable of touching people's lives in a personal and powerful way.

Bruce Springsteen is what John Lennon fought for ten years to become: a demythologized pop artist. Bruce, "the Boss" to many, is luckier than the Beatles in that he came upon the scene (1973) at a time when the politics of revolution had extricated itself from rock music. Springsteen could develop as an artist without the pressures of ideology confusing the issue. In his life and in his music, Springsteen exudes positiveness and sincerity and hope. This is the key to his success. Bruce came along when the state of the art was at its lowest. Rock had become a multimillion dollar industry with a negative image.

The days of the three hour concert had long passed. Audiences were lucky to get two one-hour sets out of the Rolling Stones, Billy Joel, and the entire bubble gum rock gestalt. Performers such as these seem no more than parodies of rock performers. Mick Jagger swings from a rope titillating the audience; Billy Joel tromps around stage in Blues brother garb, trying to make his inane lyrics sound like the real thing. Bob Dylan, representing folk and folk-rock from the 1960s, is too caught up in the aloofness of his own myth to truly communicate to an audience. Then finally, there is the fascination with rock as a destructive force: Jim Morrison and the Doors, Jimi Hendrix, and Janis Joplin represent the worst aspects of rock yet they periodically enjoy revival. In the midst of all this, Springsteen has emerged like the sane fool in a castle of insane kings.

It would take too long to chronicle his genius as a musician, his humor and sensitivity as a performer, but for me, "Because the Night" comes the closest of Springsteen's songs to conveying his massive talent. The song is a combination of two influences: rhythm and blues and hard rock. Springsteen only performs the song in concert, although Patti Smith has used it in a slightly different version on one of her albums. In a driving rhythm Springsteen sings haunting lyrics with a powerful message: two people's love can transcend the pain and boredom of everyday working life. Its theme is more realistic than the Beatles' "All You Need is Love"

and better written and more powerful than any product manufac-
tured by the Rolling Stones, Billy Joel, et al.

But the greatest appeal Springsteen has is the dedication he
brings to his shows. On his 1980 tour Springsteen has played for
four hours every night. His performance at each show is the equal
of the predecessor in quality, energy and (most important of all)
fun. In a business that produces The Who-Cincinnati fiascos, a
performer that can create the atmosphere of a campus party with
20,000 people is a rarity.

Also, Springsteen has opened up the door for a new era of
rock. Performers such as Patti Smith, Blondie, the B-52's, would
not enjoy the popularity they do if Springsteen had not broken the
stifling, stale and destructive tradition that rock had followed
since the disbanding of the Beatles.

Interactions

- Make a list of Patrick's major concerns for each draft. Compare lists.
  What new material do you find in the second draft that wasn't in the
  first.
- Write a short essay in which you compare Patrick's first and second
  drafts. Share your essay with your writing group. Did you notice the
  same similarities or differences?
- Suppose Patrick's piece were part of the music column of a popular
  magazine. Write a letter in which you defend or disagree with his position. (You will need to define which magazine you are addressing.)
- Write your own response to Patrick's new writing assignment.

□   □   □

In his third draft, Patrick maintains his focus on Bruce Springsteen but chooses to place his subject in a historical context.

BRUCE SPRINGSTEEN: A ROCK AND ROLL
RENAISSANCE

Patrick McGrath

John Lennon's death has raised a lot of questions. How significant were the Beatles both musically and politically? How
much, if at all, did they affect American culture? Were they simply a product of media hype or were they the voices for millions of
youth? I raise these questions not in order to provide answers but
to show how complicated the role of rock and roll performers (of
which the Beatles are archetypal) can be. With this in mind, my ap-
preciation of Bruce Springsteen increases all the more. There

seems to be no need to apply these questions to Springsteen. His
position in American culture seems best summed up by a line from
his song "Rosalita": "I'm not here on business baby, I'm only here
for fun." Springsteen has extricated his music from politics
without becoming inane. He substitutes acute social awareness
and sensitivity (especially songs such as "The River," "Stolen
Car") for political activism, whatever that means. Though I don't
intend to be harsh, it seems Bruce Springsteen and his music have
touched people's lives, and have done more good than the bed-in of
John and Yoko Lennon and all their political protests.

I feel Bruce Springsteen represents a renaissance for rock
music artistically and psychologically. To clarify this, I must
retrace. The Beatles, unfortuntely, began a destructive phase in
rock music. John Lennon's political activism and the social up-
heavals of the 1960s led people to view the Beatles' music as weap-
ons against the "establishment." "Lucy in the Sky with Diamonds"
supposedly espoused the wonders of L.S.D.; "I Saw Her Standing
There" was an expression of free sex and teenage nymphomania. Despite the Beatles themselves contradicting these interpreta-
tions, rock music became filled with performers for whom drugs and
violence were the principal obsession. The Doors and Janis Joplin
come to mind. Jefferson Airplane and Jimi Hendrix were also part
of this trend.

This phase subsided as society subsided around 1974. Rock entered its inane phase in which both performers and audiences became cynical towards rock as an expression of youth. Rock had
simply become another industry. Performers such as Billy Joel,
Carly Simon, and the Rolling Stones not only had nothing to say,
but they said it poorly.

This phase was short lived, for between 1975 and 1978 Bruce
Springsteen grew from an East Coast phenomenon to a national ce-
lebrity. He has suffered from hype, no doubt. He was billed as the
"next Dylan"; his former manager viewed Springsteen as the next
Elvis. But he has resisted all this to produce music that is interesting, different, and most of all, fun.

Musically, Springsteen's roots are in the white music of the
early 1960s: the Animals, the Who, and of course, Elvis. Except
for the Who, Bruce Springsteen and the E Street Band is the only
group today that excels at using instruments for rhythmic background and solos, with equal vigor. In most groups, instruments
are just "white noise" behind the singer singing. Solos jump out
of nowhere in awkward fashion.

When I saw Bruce Springsteen live, I was amazed at how little
Clarence Clemons actually played. Clemons' saxophone has become
an integral part of the E Street Band sound without dominating the

entire band. In fact, all instruments are used with skill and flu-
idity that all are essential to the band's sound. Springsteen has
at times used violins and even a tuba, a testament to his willingness to innovate and seek variety.

But musical skill alone is not the reason for the E Street
Band's success. It is Bruce Springsteen: his songs and his personality. Springsteen touches upon subjects that have real significance: trying to break out of a life of emptiness and no future (as
he did in working class New Jersey); his songs are about being
alone, frustrated. But his songs are also rockers and are often
funny ("Sherry Darling," "Rosalita," "Growing Up"). There is no
performer equal to Springsteen in concert. He is acrobatic and totally dedicated to his audience. His shows average four hours per
night, and he does quite a lot of shows. Most importantly, to me, he
is without bitterness or cynicism. He has risen above media hype
and an exhaustive lawsuit to rid himself of an exploitive former
manager, to truly communicate with his audience. His concerts are
as warm and sincere as any gathering of 20,000 people can be. Bruce
Springsteen has captured the simple essence of rock and roll: it
is not to wage war against the establishment, against one's parents, or to destroy one's self. It is simply to have fun and make
life a little more enjoyable.

□   □   □

The purpose of changing perspective is to generate many possibilities for a piece by re-envisioning your ideas from different vantage
points. Patrick, for example, could choose among the three options he
had already created for himself: to continue the general direction of
popular culture or to pursue the particular focus on Bruce Springsteen from two vantage points. (He could, of course, have created more
options by scrapping the first three.)

When Patrick rewrote his assignment for a third time, he decided to revise his second version, rather than his first. In its progress
from the first draft to the third, his essay went through some striking
changes. The indictment of popular culture in the first paragraph of
the first draft shifts to an argument for the value of rock as an anti-
dote to blandness, apathy, and misguided political activism. The dramatic changes in the essay involve calculated sacrifices—a willingness
to change everything and anything in order to follow through on a
particular insight. Apparently, to Patrick, nothing he had written was
so sacred or precious that it couldn't be deleted at a moment's notice.
His revisions were motivated by his own perception of the changing
shape of his thought.

□   □   □

Writing-and-Revising Five

(a) Free-write for three minutes on a subject of interest to you. Read carefully through your free-writing and determine if you have discovered an idea that you would like to develop further. If you haven't, free-write for another three minutes and continue the process of reading and determining what you might want to say until you have an idea that you want to develop in a draft.

Write a draft of your paper. Then write another draft, changing perspective to see what new ideas and options you discover.

(b) With a second draft of any piece of writing you're working on, experiment with changing perspective. Some of the ways you could change perspective include:

Adopt the role of someone else in the story.

Argue for an opposing point of view.

Use a different technique of narration (for instance, write the story as a letter or as a first-person account).

Change the purpose of the piece (for example, rewrite a short story as an essay about ethics).

Begin writing from a different starting point. (If you began in a general way, try using a specific example. Or, begin your piece in a different point of time.)

Pretend you're writing for a specific popular magazine or scholarly journal or any other "real" publication.

Develop another aspect of the same topic (all those angles you would like to investigate further but couldn't because you didn't have enough space).

Then write another draft based on what you discovered from changing perspective.

(c) Write a paper in which you adopt a particular stance for any subject area you are working in—for example, social history, film criticism, political science.

In your second draft, change perspective in any of the ways mentioned in this chapter. (You may need to do some library research for this project.)

Read both versions to your writing group and ask them to help you determine which version holds the most promise for further development. Then write a final draft.

(d) Write a paper in which you discuss the difference between "popular" and "classical" culture. (Because the topic is so broad, you'll need to determine what aspect of "culture" you want to focus on. You'll then need to choose a form or expression of "culture" to illustrate your point.) How do you determine what is culture, what is popular, and what is classical? Read your first draft to your writing group and ask them to tell you any places that need further clarification.

Go to the library to find supporting evidence for your opinions. Then write another, more developed draft.

(e) Write an editorial about any controversial issue on the scene right now. Make sure you specify the nature and audience of the newspaper or magazine or whatever publication you choose.

For your second draft, change the publication but keep the subject the same. Now write a final draft based on your evaluation of which version is most effective.

(f) Write an autobiographical sketch for your first draft. Then, in your second version, tell the same story from the perspective of someone else—someone in the story or someone who knows about it.

Now write a final version of your autobiographical sketch based on all the new things you've discovered by changing perspective.

MEMMo

4 fFOr YoXur iNterre#sT/%!!!

Chapter 6

Becoming Your Own Reader

This paragraph is nothing more than detail and description.
I don't like it, so I will probably revise the entire format.

TIMOTHY TSENG

On rereading a piece of his writing, Tim Tseng discovered that a particular paragraph wouldn't do—it was nothing more than "detail and description." There was nothing wrong with what he wrote, but it didn't suit his purpose. There was a specific effect he wanted to create on his readers that he couldn't do with just "detail and description"; he wanted them to feel a certain way about the events he was describing. But then, too, he didn't know what he wanted to do with his writing until he actually wrote a preliminary draft.

Every time you write, you discover something to say. But you're not writing just for yourself. Writing is a process of communication, a way of sharing your thoughts with someone else and perhaps convincing them to see things the way you do. So you have something to *say,* your meaning, and you want to *do* something with what you have said, to have some effect on your reader. Thus, saying-and-doing are both at work when you write, but they're not separate activities. In fact, like writing-and-revising, they are one process, the process of communicating.

Your intentions as a writer will determine the shape your saying-and-doing will take initially. But sometimes what you think you're saying-and-doing is not what your reader thinks you are. I can remember once writing what I thought was a wonderfully witty book review that would make anyone want to rush out and buy the book. I was all ready to send it off and await a check when I happened to show it to a friend. Her reaction was, "Why do you hate this book so much? I thought it was rather good. Well, maybe I'm just not looking for the same things you are, but. . . ."

"Wait a minute," I said, "I loved it. Isn't that what I said in my review?"

"Why, then, did you compare it to the three worst examples of that kind of writing? You could have simply said. . . ."

Aha! While I thought I was being entirely complimentary, I had used a writing strategy (comparing this particular book with three I obviously thought inferior) that created just the opposite effect on my reader.

This kind of dissonance between what you're *saying* and what you're *doing* can be lurking in any writing situation. Imagine for a minute that you're writing a letter to a close friend about your experiences in a new town. You're attending college away from home—let's say, for example, in New York City. Suppose also that you're really enjoying your first semester, though you find the Big Apple a bit (if not very) scary. Your letter could be filled with impressions from your journal of the difficulties of life in New York: finding a place to live, riding the subways, narrowly escaping from a potential mugger. If you spend a lot of time discussing the negative aspects of your experience, your friend might easily assume that you're miserable, when your real point in writing in the first place was to tell her that you're really enjoying your first semester.

When you finish writing the letter, you read back over it and note how much you've said about your difficulties. Several things could be occurring here: You really wanted to talk about the problems of everyday living—which is why you devoted so much space to them. Or, you have created that effect simply by what you have written, and your real intention may still be your original one, to talk about how you did make the right decision in leaving home. Or, it could also be that in the process of writing, you discovered that maybe you weren't so happy with your decision to attend college in New York after all.

Thus, the intention you think you have initially—the effect you want to create on your reader—can change as you discover what you want to say. Saying-and-doing, like writing-and-revising anything, is a process of selecting, ordering, questioning, and changing; it governs the choices you make as a writer and determines what your writing will do to your reader. The more conscious you are of your intentions in writing and the more conscious you are of your intended reader's needs, the more effective your choice-making will be.

One way to heighten your awareness of intention and audience is to make explicit what you're trying to achieve by writing down what you hope to say-and-do in each part of a draft. You can then examine the choices you've made and determine what effects you've created.

John Polizzotto, a student writer, wrote out his intentions and his estimations about how his reader would respond to what he was saying in the following piece. He had been reading about Charles Lindbergh. In particular, he reacted to one of the tragic events in Lindbergh's life: the kidnapping and murder of his young son. Bruno Richard Hauptmann was accused of the crime and in a very controversial and sensational trial was convicted and then executed. To this day, questions persist about whether he was, in fact, guilty. John decided that he would assume the role of the prosecutor presenting his summation to the jury, proving beyond a doubt that Hauptmann was indeed guilty. A first draft of the summation follows. In the margins, John explains his intentions.

PROSECUTION'S SUMMATION TO THE JURY

John Polizzotto

1) Ladies and gentlemen of the jury, I wholeheartedly believe that the evidence which has been presented before you has clearly shown that the man who is on trial here today is beyond a doubt guilty of murder of the darling, little, innocent Lindbergh baby.

Informal, putting the jury at ease.
Telling my (prosecution's) belief of guilt confidently.

Touching at human spirit.

2) Sure, the defendant has stated his innocence. But, who are we to believe? Do we believe the testimony of a man who has been previously convicted, in fact convicted of holding up innocent women wheeling baby carriages?[1] Or do we believe the testimony of one of our nation's greatest heroes, Charles A. Lindbergh? Mr. Lindbergh believes the defendant is guilty. So do I.[2]

Showing the negative side of defendant and connecting his past with similarity of crime he is accused of now.

Showing the integrity of the father of the victim of murder.

Overall a very biased view.

3) All I ask, ladies and gentlemen of the jury, is that you look at the evidence. First, we have the evidence that the defendant suddenly became $44,486 richer since April 2. Is it only a coincidence that the ransom was paid the same night?[3]

List of evidence, all against accused. Not too much detail is given, but if I leave the jury with a series of factual pieces all against defendant, the jury will say to themselves, "Wow, there is so much going against him, he's guilty."

4) Don't forget the testimony of Mr. Whited and of Mr. Rossiter, both of whom said they saw the accused on or around February 27 in New Jersey[4] even though the accused lives in the Bronx. The kidnapping occurred on March 1.[5]

Testimony of witnesses and specialists to show that knowledgeable men also believe defendant is guilty.

5) Then we also have the testimony of Mr. Kockler, the wood specialist, who said that a piece of the ladder side rail and the attic floor where the defendant lives were once one.[6]

6) Ladies and gentlemen, if you still are not convinced of the defendant's guilt, let me bring to your attention other pieces of evidence: the fact that similar words were misspelled in both Hauptmann's diary and the ransom note is one.

Pleading to those few jurors (if any) who I have not convinced yet.

7) Also we have the defendant's own words shouting at me, "You lied to me too."[7] Was he insinuating that he had lied during his testimony? I'll let you decide that. Need I go on?

Self-incriminating evidence. Very important. Making sure jury understands significance of statement.

8) So ladies and gentlemen, I hope you believe the defendant is guilty as does Mr. Lindbergh, possibly the greatest aviator our nation has known. I also hope this intelligent jury can see through the testimony given by the defendant and the witnesses called to his defense, many of whom also have past convictions and one even was committed to an insane asylum.[8] Surely, you will find the defendant guilty as charged.

Appealing to their better judgment. Who are you going to believe?

Playing up to them. Implying that they're intelligent enough to see the guilt of the defendant.

Notes

1. "Hauptmann: Expert Traces Lumber Rings," _Newsweek,_ 2 Feb.
   1935, p. 17.
2. "Lindbergh: Flemington's Bell Tolls," _Newsweek,_ 12 Jan.
   1935, p. 8.
3. "Hauptmann," p. 16.
4. "Hauptmann."
5. "Hauptmann."
6. "Hauptmann."
7. "Hauptmann," p. 17.
8. "Hauptmann: Defendant Weeps as Greatest Murder Trial Ends,"
   Newsweek, 16 Feb. 1935, p. 18.

Bibliography

"Hauptmann: Defendant Weeps as Greatest Murder Trial Ends."
   Newsweek, 16 Feb. 1935, p. 18.
"Hauptmann: Expert Traces Lumber Rings." _Newsweek,_ 2 Feb. 1935,
   p. 17.
"Lindbergh: Flemington's Bell Tolls." _Newsweek,_ 12 Jan. 1935,
   p. 8.

Interactions

- Pretend for a minute that you're a member of the jury sequestered after the final arguments have been presented at Hauptmann's trial. You have a transcript of the "prosecutor's" (John's) summation in front of you. In order to focus your decision about the guilt or innocence of the defendant, write down your impressions of the evidence so that you can make your final decision with a clear conscience.
- The "prosecutor" thinks he has "touched at the human spirit" in his opening statement in paragraph one. Underline the places in the text that you think are intended to appeal to your emotions. Were you moved by the plea? Write a statement explaining why or why not.
- In paragraphs three and four the "prosecutor" has listed what he regards as the vital evidence against the accused. He believes that you, as a member of the jury, will be convinced of Hauptmann's guilt. Underline what you think this convincing evidence is and write a statement in which you explain whether you are persuaded on the basis of this evidence that Hauptmann is guilty as charged.
- In paragraph seven, the "prosecutor" gives what he feels is a very important piece of evidence. As a member of the jury, do you understand the significance of the defendant's statement? Would you be convinced of his guilt based on this evidence? Write a statement explaining your response.

- Using your written statements as a point of reference, decide whether or not you would convict Hauptmann of the murder of the Lindbergh baby. Now discuss your decision with your writing group. Pretending that your writing group is the jury, deliberate and come to a final decision regarding the guilt or innocence of the defendant.
- Now change roles: Pretend that John is a member of your writing group. Based on your group's response to John's paper, make suggestions to him about how he might revise his piece to better realize his intentions.
- Write your own prosecutor's summation, using the details John presented in his paper, as well as any additional information you can find on this case.

□   □   □

Writers sometimes discover, when they reread what they've written, that what they thought they were saying-and-doing when they were writing is not what they have actually said-and-done. When Tim Tseng wrote his first draft of the essay you read in Chapter 3, he realized that he simply wasn't doing what he wanted to do and therefore had to re-envision his original idea. A portion of Tim's draft and his explanation of his intentions follows:

Last Chinese New Year, our family gathered together in the living room to celebrate after a special dinner. In accordance to Chinese tradition, the eldest member of the household would have all the attention focused on him as he told stories of the family's past. In our home, no one washed the dishes after dinner. We were together singing hymns, making prayers, and studying the Bible. After that was done, my younger brothers and I sprawled over the living room carpet focusing all our attention on father. What would he talk about tonight? Grandfather? Or his experiences when he converted to Christianity? Mother sat

This is supposed to be an introduction. It's supposed to give the reader an idea of what my family is like now and lead to my father's past. I'm thinking of cutting out this entire first paragraph because I'd rather place the point of attention on one person such as my grandfather.

next to father knitting his
sweater. She listened intently
to father as he revealed some
wonderfully mysterious secrets. That night he revealed
to us about a time of great suffering when he was a child of
seven or eight.

When I was a child, I never
experienced the sufferings my
father did when he was a child.
In 1936, a great famine hit
southwestern China. Kweichow,
my father's home province, was
one of several provinces to
suffer such misery. It was reported that nearly fifteen million Chinese peasants and
farmers died of starvation. Father vividly recalls seeing
strong men collapse to their
deaths in the middle of their
tracks. People everywhere were
suffering--some just gave up
all hope. Grandfather, the May-
or of Wuchuan County, worked
ceaselessly to help them and
even sacrificed his own family's meals quite often in order to help hungry neighbors.
Father lived on two small meals
a day and was extremely thin in
those days. Father often spoke
with pride about how much care
grandfather showed towards
fellow impoverished Chinese.
Although grandfather's family
was relatively well off before
the famine, after it, the family was left penniless.

This paragraph is nothing more
than detail and description. I
don't like it, so I will probably revise the entire format.

As he reread the paper, Tim decided that he had to revamp his
entire format to create the effect he wanted. All writers need ways of
checking themselves to be sure they are saying-and-doing what they

think they are. One useful strategy is to explore your intentions the way John and Tim did.

☐ ☐ ☐

Writing-and-Revising Six

(a) Step One
Write a draft of a paper as you normally would. Then number all your paragraphs consecutively. On a separate sheet of paper, answer the following questions for each paragraph:

1. What do you intend to say? (Include a summary of what you have written.)
2. What effect do you want to create on your reader? (Explain what you want your reader to be thinking.)

Step Two
Once you've written a draft and have explained your intentions to yourself, have another reader write out what he or she feels your writing is saying-and-doing, responding to the following questions for each paragraph:

1. What is being said? (Include a summary.)
2. What effect is being created on you as a reader? (Explain what you're thinking.)

Now compare your reader's response with what you thought you were saying-and-doing.

Step Three
Rewrite your paper, trying to match your intentions with what you now feel your reader needs to know.

(b) Follow the same procedure of exploring your intentions for any writing you are doing in another context: a business letter, a short story, a scientific report, an autobiographical sketch, a research essay, a poem, whatever. If it's something for another course, so much the better.
Ask a classmate to respond to your piece of writing using the procedure outlined in Step Two above. Did his or her response correspond to your intentions?

(c) Using the procedure outlined in Step Two above, explore the writer's intentions for something you're reading—for example, a science fiction story, an article from a popular magazine or newspaper, a film critique.

Ask someone else to read the same piece you've just analyzed and explore the writer's intentions the way you did. Did both of you perceive the writer's intentions in the same way?

(d) Research a questionable verdict—for example, Sacco and Vanzetti, Ethel and Julius Rosenberg, Alger Hiss, the Wilmington 10—or an unsolved crime.

Write a paper in which you present a summation to the jury, either as the prosecutor or as the defense attorney.

Read your paper to your writing group and ask them to play the role of the jury. Are they convinced by the evidence you've presented? Rewrite your paper using their response.

(e) Interview a member of your family or some older person you know to find a story from the past. Write a paper in which you tell the story.

Now go to the library to find supporting evidence for the events you described in your paper about the story. Write another paper incorporating what you've discovered from your research.

Boynton ©

A little over eighty years ago. --
Eighty-seven years ago ---
About seven eighths of a century ago --
Eight decades and seven years ago --- -

Chapter 7

Seeing Your Writing Through Someone Else's Eyes

Why not cut the inessentials in Cohens biography? His first marriage is of no importance. When so many people can write well and the competition is so heavy I can't imagine how you have done these first 20 pps. so casually. You can't *play* with peoples attention—a good man who has the power of arresting attention at will must be especially careful.

From here Or rather from p. 30 I began to like the novel but Ernest I can't tell you the sense of disappointment that beginning with its elephantine facetiousness gave me. Please do what you can about it in proof. Its 7500 words— you could reduce it to 5000. And my advice is not to do it by mere pareing but to take out the worst of the *scenes*.

I've decided not to pick at anything else, because I wasn't at all inspired to pick when reading it. I was much too excited. Besides this is probably a heavy dose. The novel's damn good.

F. SCOTT FITZGERALD (LETTER TO ERNEST HEMINGWAY)

Can you imagine how Hemingway's heart sank when he got the above letter from Fitzgerald: "the novel's damn good" BUT reduce the opening to 5000 words? Fitzgerald's comment meant more work—rethinking, reorganizing, more writing, more reading. Yet Hemingway asked for the response and went on to revise *The Sun Also Rises* in the way Fitzgerald indicated: "My advice is not to do it by mere pareing but to take out the worst of the scenes." Why would an accomplished writer like Hemingway need a reader to tell him what worked and what went wrong in a piece of writing?

All writers eventually need to share their writing with someone else in order to see whether or not they've communicated what they wanted to. Even professional writers, who have had a lot of practice anticipating the reactions of their readers, still depend on friends, colleagues, and editors to help them determine if their work is finished, and if not, where additional effort is necessary. They ask for responses, not because they hope someone else will do their work for them, but because they want a more objective sense of what *they* must still do in order to realize their intentions. They trust their readers to give careful reactions, but they don't necessarily expect advice about what to do. Only the writer knows what he intended to say. Therefore, only the writer can determine how to change the piece so that what he's saying matches what he intended. A writer uses readers' responses as an indicator of whether or not he's on the right track. Hemingway, for example, cut some twenty pages and refocused the entire beginning of his novel. Although Fitzgerald didn't tell him explicitly to do this, Hemingway used Fitzgerald's reactions as a way to rethink what he wanted to accomplish and to determine what was crucial to the story.

Like Hemingway, you won't know exactly what your writing says until you try it out. Once you see a reader's reactions—see your writing through someone else's eyes—you can better determine what to do next. A reader might simply tell you what she has understood from your piece or may give you some idea about what appears to be missing, but it's finally up to you to determine exactly what you'll do to change the writing so that you say-and-do what you intended. In Chapter 6, you learned how to anticipate the needs of your reader by becoming more aware of your own intentions and by noticing how actual readers perceived them. Let's look at this process more closely now, this time with an eye for how you can make changes in drafts to clarify your intentions through more writing-and-revising. Deborah Laniado, a student writer, wrote a first draft of a reflective piece about a personal experience and then explored her intentions for each paragraph.

Interactions

• As you read Deborah's paper, write down in the margin a paragraph-by-paragraph description of your response to what she's saying. Then explain what influenced you to respond as you did. What exactly did she say that caused your response? Was it the way she said it? Did you expect her to say something she didn't? Did she say anything you didn't expect or that seemed to be in an odd place?

□ □ □

As I started toward Beauty Therapy's door, the receptionist, Jackie, saw me and buzzed the door so I could open it. I pushed it

open and as I walked in, I felt all eyes look up at me and all the
girls left what they were doing to focus their attention on me.

I had just come from playing tennis so I was dressed in my
white Tacchini warm-up suit with its navy and red stripes down the
sides and my new Puma sneakers. My hair was up in a ponytail with a
bandana tied under my bangs; I hate to sweat in my bangs.

I was wearing the usual thick mascara and lipstick. It was an
ordinary Friday and everybody around was on display for each other
as usual.

I hung up my Flatbush jacket and found an empty chair to sit in
until Luda was ready to give me my manicure. I said hello to most of
the girls who happened to be my friends or at least my acquaintances. After all, everybody in the community knows each other or
at least who belongs to the community.

The women and younger girls were gossiping about the most important things in life: how many carats Jaclyn's diamond ring is;
Leslie lost five pounds; Rochelle's outfit was seen in Bonwit
Teller for $500; Sharyn and Jeff were seen together three times
which means that they must be getting engaged soon; and of course
134 is the prettiest nailpolish color for this time of year.

I thought the whole scene was amusing this Friday, while I had
never before realized how trivial and silly the conversation
really was. Luda called me to sit down and she began filing my
nails.

My mind drifted for a while and I found myself wondering what
it would be like living outside the community. I wouldn't be on
display anywhere I went and I would have more privacy.

I would probably be close to my family like I am now, and we
would probably live the same exact way. The difference would be
that our lives wouldn't be open to all for discussion. We would
still have a few select friends. The difference would be that everybody around wouldn't know what jewelry my mother owned or who I
went out with.

But then who would I marry? My whole way of thinking is geared
toward the family life available only in a close, tight-knit community. We are all similar to each other: religion-wise, finan-
cially, and most importantly, we want the same things out of life.
Maybe that is why divorce is so uncommon in my community. No. I
would never be able to live outside the community. I love it and
need it too much; despite its faults. The farthest I'll ever get
from the community will probably be living in the city my first
year of marriage, and I'll probably come home to my mother's house
for weekends then too.

I was unconsciously glancing at the various nailpolish colors deciding which to choose when I heard the door buzz. All eyes

looked up to see who was entering the salon, what she was wearing, and waiting to hear what she had to say. Deep down inside, I was no different than the rest of the girls.

Interactions

- Now compare your analysis of Deborah's paper with her own explanations of what she was trying to say-and-do. (Her explanations of her intentions follow.) To what extent does your analysis correspond to Deborah's? Do you respond to the piece as the writer predicts you will?
- What suggestions would you make for revision if Deborah were in your writing group?

☐   ☐   ☐

Paragraphs 1 and 2

I'm describing going to Beauty Therapy. The reader has no idea what it is except that there are girls there. They all looked up at me when I entered the place and I felt as if I was on display. I explain my routine tennis outfit to let the reader picture the scene and comment that although it was an ordinary Friday, I felt silly this week. The reader still doesn't know why I'm describing this, so they'll have to read on.

Paragraph 3

Beauty Therapy is apparently a manicure salon and I happened to know most of the girls there because they belong to my community. I am sarcastic about the fact that those in the community know who "belongs" in the community. I think the reader will wonder "What community"? But I hope that by reading on they'll find out.

Paragraphs 4 and 5

The girls were gossiping about other girls in the community and I was out of it. It all seemed so trivial to me and the reader can see why. The girls weren't talking about anything really significant. But the reader can see from these paragraphs that the girls know a lot about each other and it must be a tight-knit community. Who they are or where they come from, the reader still doesn't know.

Paragraph 6

I wondered what life would be like living outside the community and state that it would be much more private. I assume that I would still be close to my family. This is a normal assumption involving keeping some part of my present identity.

Paragraph 7

I'm finally asking the questions that a reader would ask. What is my community? Why do I live there? It sounds like a place

where your life is an open book to all. I hope my reader will keep on
and find out why I do live here.

Paragraph 8

I stop dreaming about life outside this (unknown) community.
I claim that I will probably live there despite its disadvantages.
The reader can easily see the disadvantages, but probably has no
idea of what the community's assets are. What is the community?
Who are these people? How many members? Where do they live? How did
I become a part of the community? Why would I want to live there
voluntarily? How long has the community been in this unknown
place? What makes them a community? The reader doesn't know the
answers to these questions. My advice to myself is to either get
out of the community or come up with some good substantial reasons
to stay there.

Paragraph 9

A girl walks into the place and all eyes look up to "check her
out." I do the same. I realize that I am just like the rest of the
girls in this community. A gossip! The community sounds really
shallow in this paper and that's not what I intended.

□   □   □

Sharyn Kassin, a classmate of Deborah's (and, as it happens, a
member of the same community), also did an analysis of Deborah's paper, just as you did. Compare your analysis with hers, remembering,
of course, that different readers may respond in different ways to the
same piece of writing.

Paragraph 1

Deborah walked into somewhere ; place is not described. She is just
starting her essay. I feel confused and must read on. I guess
that's a normal feeling so far.

Paragraph 2

Deborah describes her outfit and appearance exactly and says that
in this unknown place called Beauty Therapy, everyone is on display. Really, for all I know at this point, it could even be a house
of prostitution. Why she explains her outfit in detail, I don't
know.

Paragraph 3

Deborah now says that she's in a manicure place. Friends and acquaintances are there and now she hints that everyone knows each
other in her community. This makes me think, Are the friends the
girls who are on display for each other? And what community? (even
though I know). Still, it's only the beginning of the essay, and it

hasn't really gotten off the ground yet, so I'll wait and see what happens.

Paragraph 4

There's a hint of sarcasm here insinuating how shallow these friends and acquaintances are. I still am striving to understand what she's trying to say.

Paragraph 5

This is saying that the usual conversations that used to seem normal, now seem trivial. I am now starting to see the essay beginning to focus on something.

Paragraph 6

Deborah starts to think about what it would be like to live outside her community. It would mean having more privacy. All I know is that Deborah's community has no privacy and that people are on display, with their trivial conversations. This seems like a heck of a community. Poor Deborah--what a place to live. (Of course, I know she likes living there, so that means she's not letting her reader see the good side yet.)

Paragraph 7

Deborah assumes that her family life would stay the same. How does she know this? Also, she again says that lives wouldn't be open to all for discussion and everybody wouldn't know everything. All this community sounds like is a bunch of Rona Barretts gossiping all day long. What kind of horrible community is this, anyway?

Paragraph 8

Why is family available only in a tight-knit community? There is another assumption that's not backed up. Deborah says that the people/community are all similar and she loves it and could never live without it, despite its faults. Well, all I heard about this community in this essay so far is that they're close-knit and gossipers. What are the community's good points? How many people live there? Why are they called a community? The word community is used very often, but for all I know we could be talking about close-knit, gossipy werewolves.

Paragraph 9

Deborah uses a little example to show that she's just like the rest of the girls. Looking up and waiting to hear gossip in the manicure place.

Overall Response

Well, well. Deb--I think I know what you're trying to say and it's a great idea--but look what you make the community out to be! What is "community"? How can anyone feel anything for this when everything is so vague? If you were to build and zero in on your major ideas, not on what you're wearing, then the reader might catch on

right away. What if you changed the beginning a little and said you
walked into your usual manicure place and overheard two women gossiping about someone. If you really zero in on the trivial gossiping conversation you heard in detail, the reader could understand
why you felt so annoyed. Then you could say something like how,
even though the community is this and that (but you have to explain
the community in detail so the reader can have something to hang on
to), it's still a good place to live. You could explain that despite the pressure and the competition between people, we all help
each other. You could tell how we built the center and the Hillel
School--the good points. When you said you could never live without your community as a reader I had to say "why" because, based on
what you'd said, I'd get out as fast as possible. But if you build
up an impression of the community for the reader, then the whole
thing will make more sense. I still don't see why you went to all
the trouble to describe your outfit.

□ □ □

Using both her own and Sharyn's responses to the piece, Deborah tried once again to realize her intentions. The response of the
reader provided her with a new way of seeing what she had written
and evaluating its impact and its possibilities.

Interactions

- As you read through Deborah's final draft, indicate in the margin
places where she follows her own advice and/or Sharyn's in revising.
Explain the impact of the changes on you as a reader.

□ □ □

A SENSE OF COMMUNITY

Deborah Laniado

Friday, February 5, 1982--2:00 p.m.

As I started toward Beauty Therapy's door, the receptionist,
Jackie, saw me and buzzed the door so I could open it. I pushed it
open and as I walked in, I felt all eyes look up at me and all the
girls left what they were doing to focus their attention on me.
I had been too busy to get a manicure for weeks, but this week I
managed to squeeze in the hour. I had just come from playing tennis, so I was dressed in my white Tacchini warm-up suit with its
navy and red stripes down the sides and my new Puma sneakers. My

hair was up in a ponytail with a white bandana tied under my bangs;
I hate to sweat in my bangs. I was wearing the usual thick mascara
and pink lipstick. It was an ordinary Friday and all the girls were
on display for each other as usual. The difference was in me--I
felt as if the whole scene was funny this week.

I hung up my Flatbush jacket and found an empty chair to sit in
until Luda was ready to give me my manicure. I said hello to most of
the girls who happened to be my friends or at least my acquaintances. After all, everybody in the community knows each other or
at least who belongs to the community.

The women and younger girls were gossiping about the most important things in life: how many carats Jaclyn's diamond ring is;
Leslie lost five pounds; Rochelle's outfit was seen in Bonwit
Teller for $500. Sharyn and Jeff were seen together three times
which means that they must be getting engaged soon; and of course
134 is the prettiest nailpolish color for this time of year.

I thought the whole scene was amusing this Friday, while I had
never before realized how trivial and silly the conversation
really was. Luda called me to sit down and she began filing my
nails.

My mind drifted for a while, and I found myself wondering what
it would be like living outside the community. I wouldn't be on
display anywhere I went and I would have more privacy. I would
probably be close to my family like I am now, and we would probably
live in the same lifestyle. The difference would be that our lives
wouldn't be open to all for discussion. We would still have a few
select friends. However, I strongly doubt that everybody around
would know what jewelry my mother owned or who I went out with.

I began to fancy the idea of living outside the community and
I started getting worried. Wait a minute! Why is the community so
great? Why does my family choose to live here rather than anywhere
else in the world? My mind wandered back to the beginning.

The "community" started about seventy years ago when my
grandparents, along with many other Syrian Jews, left Syria and
immigrated into the United States. They all came penniless, since
conditions were terrible in Syria at that time and they could
rarely sell their homes or furniture if they were leaving the
country. Many owned nothing but the shirts on their backs--liter-
ally.

These Syrian immigrants started their new lives in the lower
East Side in New York. They began as peddlers of the textile indus-
try--they sold linens, tablecloths, towels. Since they were very
poor, most of the Syrians worked six days a week (they didn't work
on Sabbath--the day of rest), from early in the morning until late
at night. Their ambition, along with G-d's help, caused them to

build up their financial status gradually. Soon these Syrian Jews
were able to move to a nicer neighborhood in Brooklyn. Those Syrians who became wealthy invested or loaned their money to other
Syrians. After many years of hard work, the Syrian "community" became very wealthy.

These nouveau riche people changed in certain ways, as would
be expected, but they never forgot the important elements that
kept them together. The synagogue never ceased to play a major
role in the Syrians' lives--the Chief Rabbi married their children and he would teach and lecture the community about some new
topic every Saturday in synagogue. The synagogue would hold
drives every so often in order to raise money to build a yeshivah
exclusively for the Syrian children. After much effort and money
donations, Magen David Yeshivah was established. It is this
school that ensured the educating of the youth in the manner de-
sired. Basic tenets of Judaism were taught as well as Syrian cus-
toms. The Syrian method of praying differs from that of other
Jews--in melody and even in the pronunciation of many of the He-
brew letters. Magen David helped keep many traditions that without it would definitely have disappeared.

The community continued to live in Brooklyn, except by now,
many families were able to renovate or redecorate their homes,
thus enhancing the beauty of the area.

The most important factor that kept the Syrians together was
the shunning of intermarriage. According to Jewish law, a Jew can
marry any Jew. The Syrians tend to take this law one step further.
They even frown upon a Syrian marrying a Jew from outside the community. This may sound snobbish or narrow-minded, but this key
factor seems necessary to maintain the Syrian traditions and cus-
toms: the spicy food; the Syrian tradition of naming the first
born son after the father's father and the first daughter after
the father's mother; the phrases in Syrian that became part of
their everyday conversations. All this sets the community apart
from others.

Now, seventy years later, the community has grown tremen-
dously. Approximately 35,000 people belong to the community.
There are various new schools, synagogues, and Syrian stores to
accommodate this quickly growing group. A recent addition is a
Community Youth Sports Center--a new place for Syrian youth to
congregate and meet.

The other day my sister Michele came running home from the
center screaming, "Mom, I just met the most gorgeous hiloow (handsome; sweet) boy and he asked me out! His name is Michael Franco.
Can I go? Please?" At the mere mention of his name, my mother fig-

ured out who his family is. She teased my sister and said, "Is that the Michael Franco who has two brothers, one sister, and he lives a couple of blocks away from us?" My mother knew more about the boy than Michele did herself. Of course, a Syrian girl must spend a great deal of time with a boy before she gets married, but a great advantage of the community is that it eliminates a lot of the preliminaries that other people must go through. There are usually no "deep dark secrets" that we find out about later. Maybe that is why divorce is so rare in the community.

I stopped myself and thought--how can I have ever doubted the community? This is the only place I know of where I would want to raise a family. We are protective of one another. I love the community and need it too much; despite its faults. My G-d! With so many women living so close to each other, who know so much about one another, how can there not be gossip? As of now, I think that the farthest I'll ever get from the community will probably be living in the City my first year of marriage, and I'll probably come home to my mother's house for weekends then too.

I was unconsciously glancing at the various nailpolish colors, deciding which to choose, when I heard the door buzz. I watched all eyes look up to see who was entering the salon, what she was wearing, and waiting to hear what she had to say. Deep down inside I was no different than the rest of the girls because I too looked up.

Interactions

- How has the emphasis of the piece changed? What is your sense now of the community where Deborah lives and of her attitude toward that community? If she were in your writing group, what would you suggest as possible further changes in future revisions?
- Write a paper focusing on a community or group to which you belong: a neighborhood, a club, an extended family, a church. You may want to deal with a group to which you once belonged but have now left behind for some reason. Think of what your reader would have to know in order to get the real flavor of what being among these people is like.
- Analyze your first draft paragraph by paragraph. Ask a classmate to do so also. Compare your analysis with that of your reader and revise your paper.

☐   ☐   ☐

When Deborah revised her paper, she didn't use Sharyn's responses as a set of directions about what to add or what to leave out.

Rather, she used Sharyn's responses as a point of departure, a way of re-seeing what she had written and of determining what she should do next. She used Sharyn's suggestions, not as a rule to follow, but as a stimulus for new thought. Often, inexperienced writers fall into the trap of "just doing what they are told." They want their readers to tell them what to do. Although readers can make suggestions (like Fitzgerald did), the writer must stay in control, because only the writer knows what she wants to say. Readers can tell you what they think you have done, and different readers may tell you different things. That's why only you can determine what you should do to change your writing. There are no formulas, no easy answers.

All writers need responses, all kinds of responses—written analyses and spoken reactions. Spoken responses are often as valuable to a writer as written ones: They are spontaneous and fresh; written ones are usually thought out and thorough. Those spontaneous reactions help you to generate ideas very rapidly, to see right away what a reader thinks about your work. When you receive spoken comments, you should not only attempt to answer the reader's questions but also write down what the reader is saying. That way you will have a record of the reader's reactions and can later distinguish idiosyncrasies in the reading from real problems in the writing.

One of the best ways to get immediate response is by reading your writing out loud to other writers. Maria Maggenti, a student writer, was a member of a writing group and used their responses to develop a journal entry into a completed paper. Here's the entry.

Just a minute ago, I was in Gristede's buying a Coke when I saw a man taking a 7-Up from the refrigerator and putting it in his pocket. Then he was in front of me in line at the register and he paid for one 7-Up but the other was snuggled away. I could see into his jacket and the top of a little vodka bottle was peeking out. Those tariff labels are all the same. Then I saw him in the elevator and he was obviously very inebriated. He began to shout GOING UP! and he stood in the middle of the elevator with his feet in second position parallel trying to stabilize himself. I felt strange. Should I have said something at the store? I just winced when I saw him stick the soda in his pocket and I felt a flash flood of remorse, compassion, and anger. I fought the urge to be righteous. Am I a coward? Or am I just tired?

Interactions

• Read Maria's journal entry out loud to members of your writing group. Together suggest ways that the piece could be expanded into a paper.

□   □   □

What follows is a transcript of the responses Maria's writing group made to her journal entry.

Simone: Was there only one incident like that? The first one
          you've ever had like that?

Maria: Yeah.

Joe: But did it occur to you that . . .

M: Yeah, right before class . . .

J: that the guy might be really poor?

M: Oh! Yeah, I thought about that too, but . . .

S: If you were revising that, would it be as spontaneous?

M: Well, I know what I'd do--I'd elaborate a lot. I'd de-
         scribe what the man looked like; I'd change the tone and
         . . .

J: But what about the frantic thoughts, the moment, what was
         going through your head while it was happening. You
         weren't _thinking_ about what he was wearing, were you?

M: No, that's true, but I . . .

S: Then, uh, your only impression was that he was being a
         thief?

J: What bothered you was that he stole it?

M: Not just that.

J: Didn't it bother you that he was an alcoholic?

M: Well, my concentration was on how I dealt with the man. My
         choices. I could have said something to the man at the
         cash register. But I didn't.

S: Would it have scared you to do that?

M: No, I've dealt with it before--people who've stolen.
         Like when I was in high school, these guys I knew, they
         were vandalizing and stealing stuff and I went and told
         them that I thought that was really crass and they were
         going "Oh, Maria, you think you're so righteous" and like
         that and so I talked to my teacher and he said he'd done
         something like that once--telling someone to stop rip-
         ping stuff off and the next day he got his tires slashed.
         But this thing--well, I could go at it a few ways . . .

J: You could dwell on the feeling.

Laura: What about the thing with the vandals in your school? Does
         that fit in somewhere? I thought that was interesting.
         But would it change the focus?

M: It would get back to--an open letter to myself about guilt
         and being cowardly and choice. That would be a fine ap-

proach except I don't like the idea that writing is self-referential. Do you know what I'm saying? All those papers that are just "I this" and "I that" and so on. It's so boring to read that sort of stuff.

J: The reader could learn a lot from your feelings. He can see how it is for others.

S: Yes. Everyone asks themselves the same question in that situation--should I? shouldn't I?

M: Yeah, I guess. Well, I have to think about it. I'm not real sure about how I want to do it yet.

Interactions

• Compare your responses to Maria's journal entry with those of Simone, Joe, and Laura. What similarities and differences do you notice?

□   □   □

While Maria and her writing group were discussing her journal entry, Maria jotted down these notes:

```
Elaborate
Describe what the man looked like
Use the vandalism episode as example?
```

Although they're only notes, they were just enough to jog Maria's memory about what her group members had said to her. Later, before she actually began to rewrite the piece, she made more detailed notes to herself:

```
Tone--------like a child,
            first person*
            third person
          intellectually analytical
          a diary entry, talkative*
          journalistic approach
            --Hemingway?--
          a chronicle of an event

Point of view---reflective
              curious,* but not judgmental*
              disinterested,

              philosophical/sociological
                implications of the situation
```

```
Details-----spend time on
              description of man,
           on surroundings
           make pictures, images (little detail)
              (dialogue? none)
              inner dialogue? slight

Message----stated
              unstated*
           allow reader to draw conclusions*
           conclude myself
```

*Indicates choices I made.

Again, these notes are for Maria—to help her keep clearly in mind how her readers reacted to her journal entry and to help her generate new options for the piece. Then she wrote the following draft of "To Take," based on her own reflections and the feedback of her writing group.

TO TAKE

Maria Maggenti

Today I went to the deli to buy an orange juice and while I was over at the big glass refrigerator deciding between Tropicana or Dell fruit juice, I helped a man who had dropped a few cans of soda on the floor. As we picked them up I noticed that the man put a 7-Up soda in his pants pocket. He also held one in his hand. He got up in a hurry and walked away. I wondered if maybe this man had just stolen a soda, but I concerned myself with choosing the right orange juice. A moment later, I was in line waiting to hand over my fifty cents when I noticed that this man was in front of me. At his turn, he put seventy-five cents down for the one 7-Up while the other stayed snuggled in his pocket. The tip of a vodka bottle peeked out from his inner jacket pocket and I stared at him while I paid the cashier and he walked out into the street. On my way to class a few moments later I heard some unintelligible shouting near the elevators in another hall. I took the long route to class so that I could see what was going on. In the middle of the hall in front of the elevators there stood the man I had seen in the deli. He was screaming at the people who had gathered to look at him and he had his feet in second position parallel so that he could stabilize himself while he yelled. Even from where I stood I could smell the liquor. It was as though he was breathing a monsoon of vodka. His clothes were soiled and his glossy black hair was matted. Against

his dark skin his teeth glowed white. I stood there for a moment and
thought about what had happened in the deli. I then checked my
watch. Late for class. I turned and walked away.

When she finished her draft, she wrote this entry in her journal:

In rewriting this piece, I wrote down some notes to myself. I asked
myself some questions and tried to answer them because I felt as
though this little sketch could have gone many ways. (In fact, it
is not finished for I should at some time like to explore other ways
of approaching the piece.) The things with an asterisk are those
elements I decided to use in the piece as a whole, though I wasn't
totally sure of my method until I began to write. Often my notes on
a piece I'm working on are longer than the actual composition because I am interested in trying to zero in on what I want to do. What
happens when the composing actually starts is always a mystery,
but in providing some guidelines for myself, in exploring what the
possibilities are, I find I am less inclined to ramble on or get
stuck in a muddy literary pit.

Interactions

• Compare the responses of Maria's writing group with her notes, her
  journal entry, and her draft. Point out where in the text she used her
  group's responses to re-envision her journal entry. In the journal entry Maria said she felt "a flash flood of remorse, compassion, and anger." Do you find any place in the text where Maria shows these
  feelings? If so, where? If not, where could you suggest she add her feelings?
• Read an entry from your own journal to members of your group and
  ask them for ideas about how the piece could be expanded. Take notes
  on their suggestions.
• Use the responses of your group to develop a journal entry into a longer piece. Also write down the process that you went through to develop the piece. Keep a record of how you used your group's responses.

□   □   □

The point of sharing your work is obvious—only by getting a
reader's response will you know what you have actually conveyed to
that reader. And if you value the reader's reactions—as Hemingway
valued Fitzgerald's—you'll be able to see new possibilities and new directions for your ideas. By experiencing your language and perceptions through someone else's eyes, you'll see just how writing is a

dialogue; you'll be engaging in the give-and-take of real communication.

Writing-and-Revising Seven

(a) Read aloud to your writing group a draft of a paper that you're working on (you may want to photocopy the piece for each member so that they can follow along). Have each member respond to your paper simply by telling you what he or she thinks you've said. Take notes on each member's response. Read the paper again, asking members to take notes on:

1. words, phrases, or parts of the text they found particularly effective
2. places where they saw your intentions the most clearly
3. places where they may have gotten confused
4. points where they'd like more information
5. questions they have which the ideas in the paper raise

Discuss each reader's reactions and take notes on those things you may want to consider when you write another draft.

Write another draft of your paper and write a journal entry in which you discuss how you used, or why you did not use, the responses of your writing group.

(b) Bring in something you are writing outside of class, perhaps an assignment for another course. Talk to your group about strategies you might use to get started. Once you have a draft, read it to your group members for their responses (you may want to use the response suggestions provided above).

(c) Interview a working writer—student or professional—to determine influences on his or her work. You should ask the writer who, specifically, influenced his or her work—teachers, editors, colleagues, collaborators, friends. You may want to ask whether he or she will show you early drafts with readers' comments or discuss with you how readers have helped shape a particular piece of work.

Write a paper in which you discuss the influence of readers on the writer you interviewed.

Chapter 8

Using Responses of
Experienced Readers

As usual you lean to the unduly harsh. Your opinion of Kipling's faults would carry more weight if you could appreciate without any niggling qualifications such masterpieces as "The End of the Passage," "The Incarnation of Krishna Mulvaney" and, best of all perhaps, "The Man Who Would Be King."

Kipling is no favorite of mine—I am a pianola that often resents the music it plays—but we should all be heartily grateful for the mere vital energy of this immature middle-aged man in a feeble era of literature.

Although it is a great pleasure to see that you can at last swing several sentences, each growing out of the one before, you must now be on your guard against becoming pompous, orotund, and voluminous.

CHARLES TOWNSEND COPELAND

When a teacher comments on your writing, you should be able to use the responses in two different but related ways—as an indication of how effectively you have met the expectations of an experienced reader, and as a guide for possible revision. Even when the teacher is commenting on a final draft, you should still think in terms of revision, of ways that the piece could be changed, especially because most academic essays are "pressure-cooked" rather than "simmered," inevitably affecting the texture and flavor of the writing.

Although a teacher's comment on an intermediate draft may seem to be more *immediately* useful, comments on final drafts can have long-range impact. Consider Professor Copeland's comment quoted as the headnote of this chapter. Copeland made it on an essay about Rudyard Kipling that T.S. Eliot wrote while he was a junior at

Harvard. From Copeland's comment, Eliot could have made, perhaps did make, certain generalizations about the appropriate stance of a literary critic and about potential hazards in his writing style. Copeland, for example, says bluntly that Eliot "as usual lean[s] to the unduly harsh." And he all but scolds Eliot for his failure to "appreciate without any niggling qualifications" those of Kipling's works that could be considered masterpieces. Indeed, there is even an element of playful sarcasm in the comment, for Copeland is apparently paraphrasing Eliot when he refers to "the mere vital energy of this immature middle-aged man in a feeble era of literature." The stress that Copeland places on Eliot's style indicates clearly that he thinks Eliot ought to be conscious of how he uses language. Thus, Copeland evidently intends his comment to have an application to all of Eliot's writing, not just to this one essay. Overall, the comment both sums up Copeland's response to the essay and moves beyond the particular assignment to larger considerations—specifically, Eliot's excessive harshness and heavy-handedness.

Eliot, however, did not have to swallow Copeland's criticism whole. It was his prerogative and responsibility to reflect on what Copeland said and to decide whether the criticism was legitimate or unwarranted. In this instance, he found that he agreed with Copeland's assessment and, had he rewritten the paper, he would no doubt have been more generous to Kipling as well as more cautious about being "pompous, orotund, and voluminous." But Copeland could not—and did not—force Eliot to change what he wrote. He merely provided a young writer with a fresh perspective and an informed, sensitive reading.

An experienced reader's response is an invaluable resource to a writer. Not only can an experienced reader help you see your subject differently, noting points you may not have considered or ideas you may have skimmed over too lightly, but he or she can also bring the judicious wisdom of impartiality to your writing. When you're involved in a writing project, you're submerged in your own language and ideas. It's almost impossible to distance yourself sufficiently to sense how your intended reader will react. An experienced reader, assuming the role of that intended reader, can help you estimate the effect you've created. He or she can also help you discover effective writing-and-revising strategies and provide the continuing supportive feedback that writers thrive on.

In the following piece, Brian Santo, whose writing process paper you read in Chapter 2, was able to discover what he wanted to say as a result of his teacher's comments, which acted as a sort of catalyst for his ideas. Here's a draft of Brian's essay, followed by the comments the teacher made.

1)   Autumn in western New York is just as pretty as autumn in New
England; it just doesn't get the same publicity. The sky goes
blue-gray and the maple leaves turn. The Genesee River runs a little rougher, a little faster due to the rains of the season. Seneca
Park's visitors change from city kids who use the pool to escape
summer heat and families on a day's visit to the zoo, to suburban
kids running to get in shape for cross-country season and couples
enjoying the season, hand-in-hand, kicking through the fallen
leaves, looking into the river gorge to watch the water rushing
toward Lake Ontario. This is where and when Margaret decided to
kill herself.

2)   A description of Margaret is in order, I think. Perhaps a description of her life, her family. Something about her friends,
too. There's not much to know about her. Few people knew her, maybe
no one really did, but knowing the circumstances surrounding her
life might help, might give a person a grip on why.

3)   Simply speaking, Margaret was homely. She had an athletic
build, but never got into sports. She never really got into anything to speak of. She was always pale, with a wan smile that was
never very convincing. Not incredibly smart, no talents or skills
anyone knew of, the type of person that doesn't get much attention, not because she was invisible, but because nobody really
wanted to give her any.

4)   Was that the reason she killed herself? Because she couldn't
stand herself? Couldn't live with her inability to relate to others? Couldn't live with her inability to do anything fulfilling?
Yet there are millions of people, I suspect, who grew up much the
same way, people who never felt compelled to end their lives, who
lived a life and died peaceably.

5)   Her friends: a girl named Linda, a homosexual named John, a
bisexual named Chuck. Linda was the transient type of person who
never moved physically, but you always knew she was always someplace else, not the type of person one could get close to. John was
another face in the crowd to everyone else, to Margaret he seemed
to be the face next to her in a crowd. Chuck was always trying to get
his friends to indulge him in putting up with, and sometimes participating in, his stupid little depravities.

6)   She was a senior in 1979. She had this hopeless crush on a boy
the grade below her. True to form, the affection wasn't returned.
She and John and Chuck would get drunk and they'd cruise by the
kid's house and Chuck would get her to moon the house. Chuck always
talked about "what a great body Margaret had," and he'd practically drool when describing her in a bathing suit. He'd touch and fon-
dle, make suggestive comments and she'd smile. No one could tell
what she really felt about that; her smile was never convincing.

Maybe she knew that Chuck was just a young dirty-old-man, maybe not.

7) Could her friends, Chuck in particular, have driven her to take too many Valium? I rather tend to doubt it. Even with nuts like Chuck as friends the most a friend could usually do is prompt one to make new acquaintances to get away from them.

8) Her family? Of Polish descent, her parents were both educators; not exceptionally loveable people, but many people aren't. She had a younger brother Tom, sarcastic, negative, but very intelligent. Another sister, Jane, pretty, popular, and bright. That doesn't seem like much to provoke a suicide. Her Mom and Dad may have been somewhat indifferent; perhaps even slightly partial to her brother and sister, but that's nothing that hasn't happened to anyone else. Jane had her own life and her own interests, Tom may have directed his sarcasm at her from time to time, but other people have lived with that.

9) Well, there it is, Margaret's life. Within herself there was nothing to boast of, no shining qualities. Her friends weren't much of friends, really. Her family life wasn't depressive, but it wasn't supportive either . . ., overall, not a great life. Not emotionally equipped, unable to handle her own inadequacy, and being dealt with mostly indifference, that might convince some people to commit suicide.

10) So one night she walked into Seneca Park, swallowed a bottle of pills, and died.

11) I learned of her death from my mother. "You knew her, didn't you?" she asked me. The first thing I thought of was Chuck telling proudly of how he convinced her to moon my house as they cruised by, telling me she really liked me. I began to feel responsible, then quickly assured myself it wasn't my fault. "Isn't it terrible," my mother said, "it's not as if it was an accident; she was in control."

12) A funny idea. <u>Was</u> she in control? I'd never find an answer, the only person who could tell me was not in any condition to do so. Rather morbid, I admonished myself, feeling guilty for more than just the thought. Too late, though, the tiny American tragedy was all over now.

13) Or so I thought. Two days later I heard her boyfriend (What boyfriend? She had a boyfriend?) was found in Seneca Park trying to swallow a bottle of pills. "Let me go," he was said to have screamed, "Don't you see? We were going to be married! And if this is the way she wanted to go, so do I!"

14) She had someone who loved her and she killed herself. I didn't understand that then and I don't now. I had her suicide all reasoned out, sketchily, but I thought I understood why.

15) I guess not.

□   □   □

Brian,

By beginning your story with a description of autumn in Western New York, you provide a setting that works on a metaphysical,
as well as an actual, level. (Nature and changing seasons can be a
mystery, just as her decision to kill herself is ultimately inex-
plicable.) The character of Margaret is also multidimensional:
She has some significance for you, while at the same time, I imagine that most people have known someone who did what she did--
again, for no apparent reason.

The strongest part of your story, your treatment of Margaret,
is how you show that there <u>were</u> no obvious causes. And yet something was clearly wrong--perhaps something that could never be
verbalized.

Right now, I think you have a good frame for what could be a
powerful piece of writing. For instance, the scene between Chuck
and Margaret is quite effective. Perhaps add more scenes like
this--more explicit background information. I've indicated a few
places where further development would help me better understand
the events and characters of the story.

Paragraph 4: Where did she grow up? Under what circumstances?

Paragraph 5: These people do not seem real to me because I don't
know much about them.

Paragraph 7: She took the valium in Seneca Park? (Seems like
<u>drowning</u> is what your reader would have anticipated from your
first paragraph)

Paragraph 8: Is Jane important to your story? If so, I need to know
more about her.

□   □   □

Now read Brian's final draft. As you read through the text, refer
back to the teacher's comments. Note in the margin any changes
made in response to the comments and speculate about what Brian
did to meet the expectations of the experienced reader.

<u>MARGARET</u>

Brian Robert Santo

Autumn in western New York is just as pretty as autumn in New
England; it just doesn't get the same publicity. The sky goes
blue-gray and the maple leaves turn. The Genesee River runs a little rougher, a little faster due to the rains of the season. Seneca
Park's visitors change from city kids who use the pool to escape

summer heat and families out on a day's excursion to the park zoo,
to suburban kids running to get in shape for cross country and couples enjoying the season, hand in hand, kicking through the fallen
leaves, gazing into the river gorge to watch the water rushing toward Lake Ontario. This is where and when Margaret decided to kill
herself.

A description of Margaret is in order, I think. Perhaps a description of her life, her family. Something about her friends,
too. There's not much to know about her--few people really knew
her, perhaps no one did--she was the type of person where it seemed
that the situations and circumstances of her life were her. Looking at what happened in her life, understanding what it must have
been like to live her life, might help, might give a person a grip
on why.

Bluntly, Margaret was homely. She had an athletic build, but
she never got into sports much. She never really got into anything
to speak of. She seemed to drift about, pale, sometimes flashing
an unconvincing, wan smile.

Not exceptionally smart, no talents or skills anyone knew of:
everyone else seemed to excel at something: cooking, math, pho-
tography, writing, conversation; Margaret lived without being
recognized for anything. She was the type of person that doesn't
get much attention, not because she was invisible, but because few
ever had any reason to give her any.

And she must have been aware of all that; must have felt unneeded, unwanted.

So was that the reason she killed herself? Because she didn't
like herself? Because she couldn't relate well to people? Because
she couldn't live with her inability to do anything fulfilling?
There are millions of people, I suspect, who have felt this way at
one time or another, people who've never felt compelled to end
their lives, living and dying peaceably . . .

So what was it about Margaret that made her different, would
make her able to take her own life? Her social life?

Not that she had much of a social life. She had only a few
friends: a girl named Linda, a homosexual named John, a bisexual
named Chuck. Linda was the transient type of person who never
moved physically; she just seemed to always be someplace else; not
the type of person one could get close to. John was another face in
a crowd to everyone else, for Margaret he seemed to be the face next
to her in a crowd. Chuck was always trying to get his friends to
indulge him in putting up with, and if he could manage it, participating in, his stupid little depravities.

Margaret was a senior in 1979. She had a hopeless crush on a
boy the grade below her. True to form, the affection wasn't re-

turned. John and Chuck would get her drunk and they'd pile in a car
and cruise by the kid's house and Chuck would convince her to
"moon" the boy's window. One of Chuck's favorite topics of conversation was "what a great ass Margaret has," and he'd seem on the
verge of drooling when describing her in a bathing suit. Chuck introduced her to a friend of his who used her then never saw her
again; Chuck knew it would probably happen. Inexplicably, she
never showed any outward sign of hate, anger, contempt, rejec-
tion--only the weak smile or no expression at all. And then Chuck
was back, smiling, fondling, lewdly commenting, a young dirty-
old-man; it must have been hardly bearable.

Was that the reason she committed suicide? I tend to doubt it.
Even with nuts like Chuck as friends the most that might be an in-
ducement for is finding new friends. Or was she too insecure to try
that? Her family, it's true, didn't seem too supportive.

Her parents were academicians, strait-laced, rigid, and
strict. She had one younger brother, a junior, and a younger sister, a freshman, at the same high school as Margaret. Tom was an
intelligent kid, but clumsy socially. He was cynical and sarcas-
tic--sort of. His barbs were obviously meant to be sarcastic, but
they lacked wit and came out as mere cruelties. Margaret was surely the butt of his "jokes" quite often. He'd been heard to gloat
over his far superior SAT score or grade reports by saying just
that to her. Jane was four years younger, for all intents and purposes, in an entirely different generation. But even in the un-
likely event that Margaret would go to her kid sister for advice,
Jane probably wouldn't have been around. Pretty, intelligent,
and active, Jane was definitely the most popular of the three--a
cheerleader, an "A" student, a volleyball player, a class offi-
cer. Comparing herself to her sister, it would be obvious Margaret
hadn't as much to offer. And it would be foolish to think her parents didn't feel much the same way--people react to their children
as people too, and it wouldn't be unfair to say that Jane, if not
both she and Tom, were their favorites. Not that they loved any of
their children any more than any other, but Margaret must have
been aware of what her status was.

Reason to kill oneself? Every family with multiple siblings
is in some way similar to the one described above, so what was different? What made Margaret any different from anyone else? Was it
something outside of her--the things that happened to her, or was
it something inside of her--what she herself was or wasn't? What
made Margaret walk into Seneca Park one night, look at the river
hundreds of feet below, then swallow a bottle of valium?

I learned of her death from my mother, of all people. "You
knew her, didn't you?" she asked me. The first thing I thought of

was Chuck, proudly telling me how he got her to moon my house one night as they cruised by. How stupid it seemed then and how pitiful it was now. . . .I began to feel responsible, then assured myself quickly, sincerely, that it wasn't my fault. "Isn't it terrible," my mother said, "it's not as if it were an accident; she was in control."

A funny thought: <u>Was</u> she in control? Was it Margaret couldn't live with Margaret anymore, in which case the answer is "yes"? Or was it Margaret couldn't live with the people who comprised her family and friends, the unwittingly cruel Tom, the stupid Chucks in her life, in which case the answer is no? Was it both--what's the answer then? What else could it have been? A suicide's life must be hopeless from beginning to end, or so they must think, in order to do something so final. So Margaret's existence was not so great, and rather than bother to be a bystander in her own life, she ended it. A tidy little summation, a clearcut explanation, but I fear it isn't quite satisfactory in a classic journalistic sense, there's only four of the five W's--who, what, where, when--answered definitively. "Why" is a question that can be answered only by one person and she's not in any condition to do so. It was, and is, too late, simply too late, and a tiny American tragedy is forgotten, over with.

Or so I thought. Two days later I heard her boyfriend (what boyfriend? she had a boyfriend?) was caught in Seneca Park trying to swallow a bottle of pills. "Let me go!" he was said to have screamed, "Don't you see, we were going to be married! And if this is the way she wanted to go, so do I!"

She had someone who loved her and she killed herself. I didn't understand that then, and I don't now. Before, I knew why she did it, in a way. A "why" based on a shaky foundation of incomplete knowledge and assumptions, but yet a plausible reason, a valid set of excuses for killing one's self.

But not anymore. And because of that, it's still not over. It still isn't finished, not for me it isn't. Because there is one more question, one more unanswerable question that will probably bother me for quite a long time. Because from here it looks as though there are no reasons, just actions, and that's why the question is so scary:

Who else might disappear out of my life the way Margaret did?

Interactions

- As Brian revised his piece, his perceptions of Margaret changed significantly. Write down what you think his perceptions were in the first draft and what they became in the second. Share your comments with the other members of your writing group to see if they noticed the same changes.

- In the margins of Brian's essay, you noted where the teacher's comments stimulated revision and you have speculated about why Brian made the changes he did. Now write down your general impressions of what you think Brian himself would say about the effects of the teacher's comments on his revision. Share your impressions with your writing group. Do you agree with each other?

□   □   □

We usually don't find out why a writer made specific changes in a piece of writing. But in this case, the teacher asked Brian to describe his reactions to her comments. What follows is his statement about his writing-and-revising process:

At first, the only significance Margaret's death had for me was that I happened to know her--next to no significance at all, really. This story would never have been written--indeed, Margaret herself would never have been remembered by me unless my mother had made the "control" comment. That stuck in my mind and I wrote it in my journal (a volume at home) and I kind of forgot it while still being bothered by that "control" question, without knowing why.

And I wrote the first two drafts without knowing why. Your comments on my second draft gave a tug at something in the back of my mind, and a week later when I finally rewrote it, I got it.

Midway through writing, Margaret became an everyman of sorts. Under the surface are the questions "How many people do we really know," and "How well do we know people"? On the surface is the question "Why"? These I hope will lead people to ask themselves if anyone can just commit suicide--no warning, just do it. The final line I hoped would cement these concepts together.

Interactions

- Now that you've read Brian's statement about the effects of his writing-and-revising process, discuss it with your writing group. How did Brian's reflections compare with your speculations as a reader?

□   □   □

When writers struggle with new ideas, their early, tentative drafts are often drafts of discovery, sketches rather than blueprints. In the following draft, Scott Edwards, a student writer, explores a variety of explanations for the existence of humor. The teacher's response is that of an experienced reader, locating in the text ideas that seem exciting, or confusing, or only partially realized, embryonic.

Can you help me visualize this?

Show me how this relates.

Like Mark Twain, I believe that "[e]verything human is pathetic. The secret source of Humor itself is not joy but sorrow. There is no humor in heaven." People are characterized by their foibles, which can be either funny or pathetic, according to your point of view. That you can hold one view as easily as the other with regard to any given situation shows the views are somehow related. But joy has nothing to do with humor or pathos. It stands alone. If Twain's assertion that everything human is pathetic is valid, then the rest of his thought is true.

What is joy?

The story of Adam and Eve is relevant here. Eve and Adam do the only thing God forbids: they eat fruit from the tree of knowledge. This, of course, angers God. He tells Eve: "I will greatly multiply your pain in childbearing; in pain you shall bring forth children. . . ." This no doubt upsets Eve, whose primary purpose probably was to have children. Adam is no more

pleased to hear: "[C]ursed is
the ground because of you; in
toil shall you eat of it all the
days of your life; thorns and
thistles it shall bring forth
to you. . . .In the sweat of
your brow you shall eat bread
until you return to the ground,
for out of it you were taken;
you are dust and to dust you
shall return." God drives them
both from Eden, putting "the
cherubim, and a flaming sword
which turned every way, to
guard the way to the tree of

I don't see   life." We see that Adam and Eve
the   don't just lose out on
connection   paradise; they suffer
between A. &   inescapable struggle, pain and
E. and Twain's   death. They also,
quotation.   unfortunately, establish a
                    pattern for man's future. The
                    clear message is that the first
                    fact of human existence is
                    pathos, that is, sorrow.

                    Life, unlike the Bible, is   Is the Bible
                    not, however, wholly pathetic.   wholly
                    We don't have to read the   pathetic?
                    entire Bible to believe that
                    it's a basically serious tome.   Are there
                    Its compilers obviously didn't   funny things
                    note anything funny in what   in the Bible?
                    they wrote. But we know from   How does this
                    living that life is not   idea connect
                    unremittingly sorrowful.   with the
                    Laughter is common.   Bible?

Yes? Explain?   A moment's reflection
                    will convince you that we laugh
This is a   mostly at foolishness, the
strong,   seeming inability to cope with
effective   a situation. How common it is
example. Give   to remember old gaffes and
me more! I   chuckle, to laugh at the
feel as though   confusion and discomfort of

I hit paydirt here--or as if you hit a nerve. The expository voice suddenly became very real and human.	the uninitiated, to see someone surprised with a pie in the face and feel merry, to giggle when the word "fuck" is used outside its accepted context! We might laugh whenever someone, even ourself, is somehow caught unaware.	
This point makes me sit up and take notice.	Yet we might cry. The line between humor and sorrow is	Why?
	blurry. Neil Simon's plays about harassed New Yorkers are seen as comedies by some, as	Show me
Show me	tragedies by others. A spilled cup of coffee can be a minor	
Ah! A keen insight--develop this further?	disaster or an ocassion for amusement. A car crash can be horrible or hilarious, as can a bag lady. Point of view alone shapes our reaction, but no matter what our reaction, someone who has lost control of	
	his situation, a victim of circumstances, is always involved. Given this, we apparently should be ever	I like this phrase
	sorrowful. How is it that we can laugh?	Your next paragraph doesn't answer this question. What is the answer?
Are you sure?	Experience shows that a sense of humor helps us survive by giving us relief from sorrow. Human life itself is foolish because we alone among all beings know that no matter how we struggle to survive we will ultimately die. There	
	must be reasons for living beyond mere survival or we, being sensible, would not bother to struggle to live.	A very acute and painful paradox.
	Humor draws on the very thing that demonstrates our pathos,	I don't follow you here.

our foolishness, and makes it
desirable. It helps us want to
live.

Sorrow, then, not joy, is   Are you sure?
the source of humor. Humor
serves to mitigate sorrow, to
balance it. Joy needs no
mitigation or balance. By
definition joy is complete in
and of itself. It cannot be
improved. Sorrow, our basic
condition, is the source of our
feelings, including humor.

Then does   Since sorrow is limited to   Who do you
humor emerge   mortal man, we alone have   have in mind?
from this   humor. In Eden or heaven or
lack?   among non-human beings life is
                carefree and untroubled. A
                sense of harmony, wholeness
                and completeness is missing
                only from mortal, human
                existence. Outside pathetic
                human life being is joyous
                rather than sorrowful, so
                there is no need for humor.
                There is no humor in heaven. It
                is ours alone.

Scott--there are some very thought-provoking moments in
this essay: the blurred demarcation between sorrow and humor;
the assertion that reaction is a function of point of view; the
reflection on death. There are also puzzling things--I find the
fall of man to be either superfluous or ineffectively integrated
into the essay. I would also like to feel the sting of more examples as vivid, though not necessarily as profane, as the one I
pointed out. I am very eager to see the final draft of this essay.

Interactions

• If Scott were in your writing group, what writing-and-revising strategies would you suggest to him, based on your reading of his text and
the teacher's comments? (Suggest at least two ways that he could re-

vise the piece.) Share your two strategies with your writing group, discuss why you proposed them, and decide which of the group's strategies shows the most promise for revision of the piece.

□   □   □

Using his first draft and his teacher's response as a point of departure, Scott changed his approach to his material quite drastically, yet still maintained his original intention of explaining his convictions about the origins of humor. As you read the final draft of Scott's essay, see if he used any of the writing-and-revising strategies your writing group proposed.

<u>RON</u>

Scott Edwards

Everything human is pathetic. The secret source of Humor itself is not joy but sorrow. There is no humor in heaven.

Mark Twain, <u>Pudd'nhead Wilson's New Calendar</u>

The line between joy and sorrow is blurry to most people; for the ironic there is none. My friend Ron showed me why. His image provoked either laughter or pity, but until we became close friends, I didn't know how to take him. On the whole he seemed pathetic, yet undisturbed by his condition. Once I knew him well I discovered he'd made his peace with the world. He was resigned to the whims of fate, and so had stricken anxiety from his life and had come to shrug off the laughter and pity aimed at him. He learned that laughter and pity were but two manifestations of attempts to deny the truth that he embodied--that life was ultimately meaningless. The pathetic, he decided, are those who fail to see that humor and sorrow are tricks people play on themselves. Irony, at once humorous and sorrowful, is nearer to truth.

I first met Ron on a wet, chilly March day in 1975 in Chicago, sitting with a mutual acquaintance in a McDonald's. He was, I later learned, thirty-eight, but I thought him at least ten years older. Balding, overweight, a bit greasy, and dressed in mismatched second-hand clothes that fit poorly, he looked like a prototype down-and-out rooming house boarder, which he in fact was. He was unemployed, living on welfare, and, as I met him, trying to cadge a free meal (and at the same time a right to loiter) from our common friend, John, a nineteen-year-old megalomaniacal street hustler.

Ron, during leaner times, was prone to live a streety life and so was known to a diverse set of people, many of whom I too came to know. His comings and goings were often discussed. The street people, mostly older juvenile delinquents, generally found him repulsive and foolish. They made fun of his looks, his age, his clothes, his home, his false teeth, and his poverty. He was known as an old clown. Among his other acquaintances, people he'd come to know during better times, Ron was mostly looked upon as a nice, if ineffectual, guy. His worth was discounted to good intentions. "He seems capable of so much more," they thought, but considered him and wondered, "What is his problem?" He cast a pall over their gatherings; they didn't want him around. He depressed them.

They all, no doubt, soon wondered what my quirk was since I began spending a lot of time with Ron. What was my problem? Well, it was similar to Ron's. We became friends because we shared related problems. I was then a naive college freshman lacking any notion of what I was or might or should be doing with my life. Ron, it turned out, had had exactly the same problem, but had long ago finished struggling with it by resigning himself to chance. He'd never had any great goals to achieve or burning passions to satisfy. Once, that had worried him, as my rudderlessness then worried me. Ron came of age without any purpose for his life and was unable to shape one. I likewise had never been able to invest my life with any overall meaning. Ron came to realize that life ultimately has no meaning because struggle as we might to live, we must eventually die. Thereafter he was free of worry and lived mostly for the present, giving the future little thought. He was a sort of modern, urban hobo. Somehow, I sensed his remedy for my anxiety, and he instinctively recognized my dilemma, and we drew close to one another.

What we shared finally was recognition and acceptance of life's absurdity. It bound us as companions. It also accounted for the reactions Ron evoked from people who knew him even slightly. The incompetent and failed street people feared growing to resemble Ron. It was only too possible. They were never prone to think about the future realistically. They all had grandiose fantasies about their future wealth and fame. Ron's being threatened them with realistic thoughts of the future. They couldn't take Ron seriously without losing their own self-esteem, so they saw him as a fool. They dismissed him and the anxiety he evoked by only acknowledging some one of his pathetic features, for example, his Porky Pig-like face, and dealing with only that aspect of him. They used laughter to preserve the integrity of their own world view when that view was threatened with contradiction. Among those who pitied Ron, they used pity for the same reason the street people used laughter--to deny Ron's reality. The pitiers were generally successful and respectful, in the traditional senses of the words (i.e., generally white collar types). They had worked hard to achieve all they had achieved, and Ron, simply by being, contradicted their belief in the worth of all they won. The accomplished needed to abstract Ron to his seediness and apparent failure so they could assume that he aspired to something more than what he had, to something akin to their own successes. What both groups failed to perceive in their cursory considerations of Ron was his self-acceptance and complacency. He had neither grandiose fantasies nor higher expectations. He thought them equally futile.

He lived as though in a state of grace, free from the worries and woes of most mortal men. He let fate, or, if you will, grace, look to his needs. At times, he resembled a dumb animal in that he needed only food and simple companionship to be fully content. He showed little emotion, having no need of humor or love or sorrow, because he had no anxieties. He might have been a heavenly being but for his earthly body.

But it was his physical appearance and material wealth by which his peers judged him when his unique point of view should have mattered most. I was lucky in being disposed to see past his outward pathos to his inner truth. When we met, I was already facing down the path he had long before taken. Nothing was ever funny or sorrowful or meaningful to me except myself. I felt emotionally dead and was sure that I needed some sort of cure. Ron showed me that I was relatively healthy while others, far more than I, were pitiful for their self-deluding emotions. By laughing at and pitying the apparent failings of their fellows, most men believed that they would achieve or had achieved something of everlasting value. But laughter and pity both serve to stave off recognition of the sorrow underlying all human existence, namely, mortality.

So Ron judged men according to their world view rather than their most apparent characteristics. He had found, he said, few who, like himself, were wholly accepting of their own mortality. There were, however, correspondingly few who could wholly deny it. Most fell somewhere between the two extremes. This, he reasoned, explained how one man's humor could be another man's sorrow. Each man, according to the manner and degree of his acceptance of mortality, would have a unique sense of humor and a unique sense of sorrow. Nowhere would they be the same between any two men. Sorrow and humor, therefore, could not be absolutely distinguished by most men. Those who persisted in trying to distinguish them were pathetic because truth lay nearer perceiving the irony of humor and sorrow being two parts of one human mechanism for survival.

Interactions

- In Scott's final draft, underline in your book the places where you notice ideas that also appeared in the first draft. Write out an explanation of how he has used new material and a new approach to realize his original intentions.
- Bring in a paper that a previous teacher has commented on. What did the teacher focus attention on? Ask your writing group to respond to it as experienced readers. What would you now do to revise the piece?
- Take a paper that you have written earlier for this course or another. Try a new approach like Scott did to see if you can capture the essence of what you want to say through a character analysis.

□   □   □

Scott's change of approach in his final draft was motivated by his realization that he could use a character sketch to convey his theory of humor. He did not take his teacher's comments as directions; he used them to refine and focus his strategies for defining humor.

Like good teachers, professional editors are experienced readers who respond sensitively to a writer's work. Editors' suggestions often lead to major revisions. For example, Max Perkins, a famous and influential editor for Scribner's, worked closely with such important American writers as F. Scott Fitzgerald, Ernest Hemingway, Ring Lardner, and Thomas Wolfe. Perkins' comments guided Wolfe in shaping *Look Homeward, Angel* from a rough, unwieldy manuscript entitled *O Lost* into its final form as a modern classic. Editors work with an author's text at every level down to the most minor word changes (which may, of course, produce major effects). But one thing a good editor absolutely never does is to change any part of the text without the author's approval. Perkins made this point quite emphatically in a letter to Fitzgerald written December 12, 1921:

> Don't ever *defer* to my judgment. You won't on any vital point, I know, and I should be ashamed if it were possible to have made you; for a writer of any account must speak solely for himself.

The role of the editor is to collaborate with the writer in making revisions. Editors, like teachers, try to imagine the reactions of the intended audience—the public—and suggest, not dictate, ways the writer can better meet the needs of that audience. For instance, Robert Brown, a professional writer, was working on an article for a local newspaper about the relationship between science and art. (You saw his preliminary map for the article in Chapter 5.) What follows is an excerpt from the draft he presented to the editor.

SCIENCE AND ART: ARE THEY SO DIFFERENT?

Robert T. Brown

"I believe the intellectual life of the whole Western Society
is increasingly being split into two polar groups. Two polar
groups: at one pole we have the iterary intellectuals . . . at the
other, scientists. Between the two, a gulf of mutual incomprehension. Sometimes, particularly among the young, hostility and
dislike, but most of all lack of understanding." So wrote C. P.
Snow in 1959. Snow, who frequented both literary and scientific
groups, was struck not only by their mutual incomprehension, but
their inability and unwillingness to communicate with each other. In recent years the gulf between the two groups has actually
increased.

There are many different kinds of knowledge, of ourselves, of
others, and of the world and universe around us, and there are many
paths to knowledge. In any absolute sense, no one path is "better"
than any other, although each will be more useful for certain purposes. Science and art are two of these paths. However, science is
particularly misunderstood, and the misunderstandings may exac-
erbate the separation between scientists and others. It should be
noted that the split between science and art is relatively recent.
Not too long ago, people excelled in many different fields that
were seen as complementary, not in conflict. Many Renaissance men
achieved greatly in several fields. Michelangelo was one. Leonardo da Vinci, in particular, was both a scientist and artist.
More recently, Jefferson and Franklin can be regarded at least as
philosophers, artists, and scientists.

The present lack of knowledge among the general public of
what science is and how it works is disturbing, particularly considering the importance of science in contemporary life. Unfortunately, many get their view of scientists from films and
television shows, which portray scientists as demented egomani-
acs for whom the end of scientific knowledge justifies any number
of inhuman means. The mad scientists, from Dr. Frankenstein
through Dr. Jekyll to Dr. No, is an all too familiar stereotype.
One of my favorites is the movie, "Sssss," about a scientist whose
self-appointed mission in life is to turn men into snakes. Children are exposed to similar stereotypes--consider the treacherous, if bumbling, Dr. Smith on "Lost in Space" and the frequent
evil scientists on cartoon shows.

Are the characteristics of science so different from other
paths to knowledge? I will describe briefly some essential characteristics of science and suggest that scientists and artists
share some important characteristics. Science may indeed be gen-

erally more cognitive and art more affective, but even this difference is one of degree and not of kind. At the outset, I should say that this paper owes much to the thoughts of two scientist-humanists, the psychologist D. S. Lehrman, and the mathematician, Jacob Bronowski.

The essentials of science have been stated frequently and can be summarized briefly. First, science assumes that there is a cause for every effect, that events are determined. This is, of course, an assumption that cannot be proven. This aspect of science is actually very optimistic: There is order, not chaos, in the universe. Events follow discoverable principles and do not occur through chance or fate. This assumption has led both to greater understanding of ourselves and our universe and to technologies that have alleviated pain and suffering.

Science is empirically based. An event must be publicly observable to qualify as scientific data. Thus, introspective data, those gained from looking within oneself, do not qualify as scientific however necessary they may be for other kinds of knowledge. In this way, science deals with reality and assumes that through research we may gain an increasingly accurate picture of external reality.

Science is public. A piece of research is not considered part of science until it is published and available to other scientists. Once published, the work is open to verification by others to ensure its reliability. Scientists, then, communicate both what they have found and the methods they have used. Because science is empirical and because the observer, human or mechanical, may affect and change the phenomenon observed, scientific knowledge holds only within certain limits of confidence or probability. Thus, science is uncertain--Scientific knowledge and theory are always open to revision. Applied formally to particle physics, this position is known as the Heisenberg Uncertainty Principle. Jacob Bronowski has suggested that a better name would the the Principle of Tolerance--we can in principle have knowledge only within certain limits of tolerance. A new finding today may render yesterday's knowledge obsolete. Thus, there is--and can be--no _exact_ science. In this way scientific knowledge conflicts and clashes with dogma. The absolutism and rigidity of political, religious, or social dogma is incompatible with the constant change and empirical nature that characterize science. When scientists have clashed with dogmatists, the scientists have ended up on the rack, at the stake, or in the concentration camps.

Perhaps most importantly, science is a set of rules which are followed by all scientists. These rules, the scientific method, state the way in which observations must be made, experiments conducted, and theoretical explanations developed. Science, then, is like a game, which like other games must be played by the rules. There are, in fact, books on sciences with titles such as, The Game of Science and The Science Game. Teaching these rules is a major aspect of training scientists, and research reports are evaluated by other scientists to ensure that these rules have been followed. Intentional breaking of the rules by faking data or misdescribing one's methods is among the worst sins a scientist can commit.

Reduced to a set of statements such as this, science may sound dry and without emotion or feeling. Not so! Science can be as passion filled as any artistic endeavor.

Interactions

- Pretend that you're the editor of a local newspaper. Reread Brown's article and make comments in the margins and/or changes in the text which reflect your responses as a reader and your suggestions and strategies for meeting the needs of the intended readers (the public).
- Compare your editorial comments with those of the other members of your writing group.
- Now assume that your writing group is the editorial board of the newspaper and you're reviewing the article prior to publication. In collaboration with your group, write a letter in which you explain what changes you feel the author needs to make in the article and why.

□ □ □

What follows is the same excerpt of Brown's draft with comments from his editor, a colleague of his who was assigned to help all faculty modify their writing to meet the expectations of the general newspaper audience. The editor put brackets around parts that he felt could be deleted from the text, and raised questions or made statements about sections that he felt would lose the audience's attention. The motive, then, of this editor was not to "fix" the writing to make it appear better for the local readership. Rather, he was attempting to stimulate Brown to re-envision his ideas.

SCIENCE AND ART: ARE THEY SO DIFFERENT?

Robert T. Brown

Delete quotation? ["I believe the intellectual life of the whole Western Soci-

ety is increasingly being split into two polar groups. Two polar

groups: at one pole we have the literary intellectuals . . . at

the other, scientists. Between the two, a gulf of mutual incompre-

hension. Sometimes, particularly among the young, hostility and

dislike, but most of all lack of understanding."] So wrote C. P.

Snow in The Two Cultures in 1959. Snow, [who frequented both lit-
                                           a novelist and scientist,
erary and scientific groups,] was struck [not only] by [their mu-
           the   *of the two cultures to understand*
tual incomprehension, but their] inability and unwillingness [to

communicate with] each other. In recent years the gulf between the

two groups has [actually] increased.

There are many [different] kinds of knowledge [of ourselves,

of others, and of the world and universe around us,] and [there

are] many paths to knowledge. [In any absolute sense,] No one path
                        another,   *is*
is "better" than [any other,] although each [will be] more useful

for certain purposes. Science and art are two of these paths. How-
                                                                        Are you
ever, science is particularly misunderstood, and the misunder-   *exagerat*
          worsen   *that already exists*   *the cha*
standings may [exacerbate] the separation between scientists and   *here? Ma*
                                        This   *it's more*
others. [It should be noted that the] split between science and   *accurate*
         was not always so.   *?*
art [is relatively recent.] [Not too long ago,] people excelled in   *say ou*
                                                                        Conflicting tende
many different fields that were seen complementary, not [in con-   *is to*
                                                                        increas
                                                                        specia

flict.] [Many] Renaissance men achieved [greatly] *recognition* in several

fields ; Michelangelo [was one.] *and* Leonardo da Vinci, [in particu-

lar, *for example, and* was both a scientist and artist. More recently,] Jefferson

and Franklin can be regarded [at least] *also* as philosophers, artists,

and scientists.

[The present] *our culture's* lack of knowledge [among the general public of] *about*

what science is and how it works is disturbing, particularly con-

sidering [the] *how* importance [of] science [in] *is to* contemporary life.

Unfortunately, many get [their] *of us? our* view of scientists from films and

television shows, which] *that* portray scientists as demented egoma-

niacs [for whom the end of scientific knowledge justifies any num- *who commit hideous crimes in order to conduct outrageous*

ber of inhuman means.] *experiments.* The mad scientist, from Dr. Frankenstein

through Dr. Jekyll to Dr. No., is an all too familiar stereotype.

One of my favorites is the movie, "Sssss," about a scientist whose

[self-appointed] mission in life is to turn men into snakes. Chil-

dren are exposed to similar [stereotypes] *distortions?* --consider the treach-

erous, if bumbling, Dr. Smith on "Lost in Space" and the *all*

[frequent] evil scientists on cartoon shows.

Yet Are the characteristics of science so different from other

paths to knowledge? [I will describe briefly some essential char-

acteristics of science and suggest that scientists and artists *Say-*

share some important characteristics.] Science may indeed [be *don't say youre going*

generally more cognitive and art more affective], *involve more thinking and art more feeling* but even this *to say,*

difference is one of degree and not of kind. [At the outset, I

should say that this paper owes much to the thoughts of two scientist-humanists, the psychologist D. S. Lehrman, and the mathema-

tician, Jacob Bronowski.] *Your audience won't understand this, or care.*

are:

The essentials of science [have been stated frequently and

can be summarized briefly.] First, science assumes that there is a

cause for every effect, that events are determined. This [is, of

unproven

course, an] assumption [that cannot be proven. This aspect of sci-

ence] is actually very optimistic: There is order, not chaos, in *Isn't*

)chance

the universe. Events follow discoverable principles and do not *)one of*

or?

occur through chance [of] fate. This assumption has led [both] to *these*

principl

greater understanding of ourselves and our universe and to tech-

nologies that have alleviated pain and suffering. *(This is such a good po*

You should be more speci

Second, *even*

Unclear to ∧ [Science is empirically based.] An event must be publicly ob-

your readers *information* *dramatic*

suggest "Science servable to qualify as scientific data. Thus, [introspective

is based on *does*

experiment data, those] gained from looking within oneself, do] not qualify

not intuition *even if it is crucial*

or untested as scientific [however necessary they may be] for other kinds of

belief" *confronts*

Follow knowledge. In this way, science [deals with] reality and assumes

directly *can?*

with "In that through research we [may] gain an increasingly accurate pic-

this way..." ture of external reality.

Third,

Science is public : [A piece of] research is not [considered]

part of science until it is published and available to other sci-

can be verified.

entists. Once published, the work [is open to verification by oth-

ers to ensure its reliability. Scientists, then, communicate

both what they have found and the methods they have used.] Because

the scientist may unwittingly

[science is empirical and because the observer, human or mechanical, may] affect and change [the phenomenon] observed, scientif- *what is being* ← (*too technical*)

ic knowledge [holds] only within certain limits of confidence or *is valid*

probability. Thus [science is uncertain--]scientific knowledge

and theory are always open to revision, [Applied formally to par-

ticle physics, this position is known as the Heisenberg Uncer- *inappropriate for your audience?*

tainty Principle. Jacob Bronowski has suggested that a better

name would be the Principle of Tolerance--we can in principle have

knowledge only within certain limits of tolerance.] A new finding *Since*

today may render yesterday's knowledge obsolete. Thus, there

is--and can be--no exact science. In this way scientific knowl-

edge [conflicts and] clashes with dogma. The [absolutism and] ri- *often*

gidity of political, religious, or social dogma is incompatible

with the constant change and [empirical nature that character- *exact proofs of*

ize] science. When scientists have clashed with dogmatists, the *Unfortunately*   *these*

scientists have ended up on the rack, at the stake, or in [the] con-

centration camps.

But Perhaps most importantly, science is a set of rules [which

are] followed by all scientists. These rules, the scientific *known as*

method, state the way in which observations [must be] made, ex- *are*

periments conducted, and [theoretical explanations] developed. *theory*

Science, then, is like a game, which [like other games] must be

played by [the] rules. There are, in fact, books on science with

titles such as "The Game of Science" and "The Science Game." *) Omit mention of books?*

Teaching these rules is a major aspect of training scientists, and research reports are evaluated by other scientists to ensure that

these rules have been followed. Intentional breaking of the rules

by faking data or misdescribing one's methods is among the worst

sins a scientist can commit.

No ¶   [Reduced to a set of statements such as this, science] may
                                                 This?

sound dry and without emotion or feeling. Not so ! Science can be
                                                            as
[a] passion-filled as any artistic endeavor.

Interactions

- Compare the editorial responses of your writing group with those of Brown's editor.

☐   ☐   ☐

After reviewing his editor's comments, Brown wrote a final draft, which was published in his local newspaper, the *Star News* (Wilmington, NC).

Science, Art, and Tolerance

Robert T. Brown

"I don't care what others do with my discoveries. I don't care what sacrifices must be made or what the cost is. Nothing can stand in the way of my research!" So says the movie scientist, in a predictably heavy German accent, as his assistants go about carrying out his research by zapping people with laser beams or testing some new exotic nerve gas on them.

The movie and television stereotype of the scientist is familiar—a demented egomaniac who commits hideous crimes in order to conduct outrageous experiments. From Dr. Frankenstein through Dr. Jekyll to Dr. No, the scientist as madman and science as somehow evil have become part of our culture. This view is also transmitted to our children—consider the treacherous, if bumbling Dr. Smith on "Lost in Space" and all the evil scientists on cartoon shows.

Science is a particularly misunderstood form of knowledge. Our culture's lack of knowledge about science and how it works, and about scientists and how they work, is disturbing, particularly considering the importance of science in contemporary life. Some years ago, British novelist and scientist, C. P. Snow, suggested that our intellectual society was split into two cultures, one scientific and the other literary and artistic, with a gulf of mutual incomprehension between them. We seem, however, to have a better and more tolerant understanding of other forms of knowledge, such as art, than we do of science.

But, are the characteristics of science so different from other paths to knowledge? Science may indeed involve more logic and art more feeling, but even this difference is one of degree and not of kind. The essentials of science can be summarized briefly. First, science assumes that there is a cause for every effect. This assumption is actually very optimistic: There is order, not chaos, in the universe. Events follow discoverable principles and do not occur through chance or fate. Because of this assumption, we have a greater understanding of the universe around us and of the mysteries of the mind. We can relieve the pain and suffering of those who in an earlier time would have been doomed to death or an asylum.

Second, science is based on observation, not intuition or untested belief. Thus, information gained from looking within oneself is not scientific, however crucial it may be for other kinds of knowledge. In this way, science deals with reality and assumes that through research we can gain an increasingly accurate picture of our world.

Further, science is public. Research is not part of science until both the findings and the methods used are published and available to other scientists. The work can then be verified by others.

Because science is based on the senses and because the observer, human or mechanical, may affect and change what is observed, scientific knowledge holds only within certain limits of confidence or probability. We can in principle have knowledge only to a degree of tolerance. Further, scientific knowledge and theory are always open to revision. A new finding today may render yesterday's "fact" obsolete. Thus, there is—and can be—no exact science. And in this way, science clashes with dogma. The absolutism and rigidity of political, religious, or social dogma are incompatible with the observable basis and constant change of science. When scientists have clashed with dogmatists, the scientists have ended up on the rack, at the stake, or in concentration camps.

Perhaps most importantly, science is a set of rules followed by all scientists. These rules, the scientific method, state the way in which observations are made, experiments conducted, and theories formulated. Science, then, is like a game, which like all games, must be played by rules. Teaching these rules is a major aspect of training scientists, and research reports are evaluated by other scientists to ensure that the rules have been followed. Intentional breaking of the rules by falsifying results or misdescribing methods is among the worst sins a scientist can commit.

Reduced to a set of statements such as this, science may sound dry and without emotion or feeling. Not so! Science can be as passion-filled as any artistic endeavor.

For what do the scientist and artist do? First of all, both create new knowledge and new ways of looking at ourselves and at our world. Further, both science and art have aesthetic qualities, and the same words—beautiful, powerful, sensitive—that are used to describe a poem, sonata, or painting, are also used to describe research and theory. Indeed, the emotion in both artist and scientist must be similar when they reflect on a completed work.

Further, an artistic work, like a scientific one, is of no value until it is presented to others. The author's "great unwritten novel" or the artist's "great unpainted painting" are of no more value than the scientist's "great unpublished experiment." Ideas are cheap; it is products that are dear. Thus, science and art are both public.

In both science and art, true creativity is characterized by those who find a new way of looking at reality—and thereby change our own view of the world. Reality exists by common agreement and is subject to change. And let there be no mistake—reality has changed several times for Western humanity over the last several hundred years. Before Copernicus, reality was that the other planets and the sun revolved around the earth, which was at the center of the universe. Copernicus changed all that, although we still talk of the sun rising and setting! Reality also changed after Darwin, Freud, and Einstein, never to be the same again. But reality also changed after Monet, James Joyce, and Stravinsky, never to be the same again. Scientist and artist each provided a new view of the way the world is put together.

Yet those views are quite different. The scientist's must be open to rigorous testing; the artist's is very much a personal view. If some artistic views are considered better than others, it certainly must be on grounds other than objective observation. An artist saying to another, "No, you are wrong; this is the way the world really is," is ludicrous. But scientists have arguments like that all the time. Some have been going on for hundreds of years.

A further difference between science and art is the scientific method that defines science. Perhaps the crucial difference is that the truly creative scientist expands our view of reality by finding a new way to follow his rules, whereas the truly creative artist expands our view of reality by finding a new way to break accepted rules.

But scientists and artists share a common bond: In neither field can there be a complete, final answer. Both constantly change; neither is exact. Both share the crucial need for tolerance of other views in order to survive; both should stand together against intolerance and dogma. Artists were in Nazi concentration camps with scientists. In Russia, artists and scientists are together today in the Gulag Archipelago.

Robert Benchley once said, "The world is divided into two parts—those who divide the world into two parts and those who do not." I prefer to be among those who do not. Art and science are both very human forms of knowledge. In the words of Jacob Bronowski, both an artist and a scientist, "We must cure ourselves of the itch for absolute knowledge and power . . . We must touch people . . ."

□   □   □

Like Scott, Brown didn't follow his editor's comments to the letter. What he did instead was to use the comments as guidelines for meeting the expectations of his intended audience.

□   □   □

Interactions

- Discuss in your writing group the writing-and-revising strategies Brown used. How did they correspond to your suggestions and to those of his editor?
- You are now the intended audience, a subscriber to the local newspaper. Write a letter to the editor in response to the article.
- Share your letters with your writing group. What are the different ways people responded to the article?

□   □   □

Writing-and-Revising Eight

(a) Choose a piece of writing you have worked on recently—one which has gone through more than one draft. Write a paper in which you analyze the process of how you clarified your original intentions in that piece of writing. In your analysis, discuss what writing-and-revising strategies you used. Consider all the resources you have had available. For instance, did you begin from an entry in your journal? If so, how did your writing change from the journal entry to the draft? Was your revision influenced by comments from your writing group? Did you use comments from experienced readers such as your teacher?

(b) Return to the Writing Profile Questionnaire in Chapter 1 and answer it again. Compare your answers now with your previous response. Have your perceptions of yourself as a writer changed? Write an essay in which you trace your development as a writer during the time you've been working with this book.

(c) Investigate the influence of public opinion on the writing of a published author. For example, Stephen Crane rewrote *The Red Badge of Courage* to make it less gloomy (and therefore more appealing), even deleting an entire chapter. (Writers affected strongly by public opinion include Kate Chopin, Theodore Dreiser, Thomas Hardy, among others.) A good point of departure for your research would be to look at a definitive biography of a professional writer and then to track down contemporary book reviews. (*The Critical Heritage Series,* published by Routledge and Kegan Paul is useful for these purposes.)

Write a paper about what you discover.

(d) Investigate the influence of public opinion on other kinds of literature—such as public documents, a piece of legislation or published scientific studies. (For instance, the 1964 Civil Rights Act underwent drastic changes, in response to pressures exerted from various sources, before it was passed in final form. Or, consider how a scientist, such as Galileo, might have been led to new discoveries by working against prevailing attitudes.) Write a paper in which you show how public opinion shapes (or does not shape) the writing-and-revising process.

Chapter 9

The Writing of *Writers Writing*

By the time I am nearing the end of a story, the first part will have been reread and altered and corrected at least one hundred and fifty times. I am suspicious of both facility and speed. Good writing is essentially rewriting.

ROALD DAHL

It's a little deceptive to talk about motives. What you do is write the book you can write—write the book you find yourself writing—and after it's done you look around for a rationale for it.

E.L. DOCTOROW

When we began to see that *Writers Writing* might actually see print—in other words, we might someday revise it for the last time—it occurred to us to share with our readers our own composing process, and what we learned about writing from writing this book. We thus decided to add an epilogue to the book we had written, a chapter we could call "The Writing of *Writers Writing*." We weren't sure, or rather we were totally confused, about how to approach this new chapter; nevertheless, we decided to begin somewhere and see what we could do. Somehow, Melinda (procrastinator supreme) first produced the first draft of an incomplete version of the story (as she viewed it). She left it unfinished because she didn't know where to go from there. For one thing, how can you finish the story before it's over? And, what might be the point of trying to explain everything anyway (even if it could be done)? We reached an impasse—a writer's block, perhaps even a false start, or worse yet, a dead-end.

Our problem was solved when we decided to leave this chapter as a draft, as something not in final form. Lil and Vara then offered their responses, also in draft form, to what Melinda wrote, and Bob Boynton, our editor, asked if he could add a few comments. What follows now is what we hope is a pretty good representation of how our collective writing-and-revising process took shape over the course of writing this book.

□ □ □

Chapter 9: Epilogue

The Writing of *Writers Writing* (First or Second Draft)

I am going to read what I have written to read, because in a general way it is easier even if it is not better and in a general way it is better even if it is not easier to read what has been written than to say what has not been written. Any way that is one way to feel about it.

And I want to tell you about the gradual way of making *The Making of Americans*. I made it gradually and it took me almost three years to make it, but that is not what I mean by gradual. What I mean by gradual is the way the preparation was made inside of me. Although as I tell it it will sound historical, it really is not historical as I still very much remember it. I do remember it. That is I can remember it. And if you can remember, it may be history but it is not historical.

—Gertrude Stein, "The Gradual Making
of the Making of Americans" (1935)

Lil: I have just read what Gertrude Stein has written that you have written of hers for me to read. I love it! Because in a general way . . . anyway that is one way to feel about it.

Vara: I love that quotation from Stein—it seems so absurd and so lovely, a perfect paradigm of the complexity of our composing process, of our own struggles with language and memory as we were writing the book.

Bob: Amen.

Like Gertrude Stein, we spent almost three years in the making of our book, but it wasn't a gradual process at all. It was gradual only in the sense that it took three years from the time the idea of doing a book first entered our heads until the time we saw it in production, that inevitable time when we could no longer make any changes. As I look over my journal for the past year, I realize that it doesn't mention how we got the idea in the first place, what led us to thinking the project might be worthwhile; instead, what I recorded is how we went about making the book once we decided to do it.

Vara: Melinda, what do you mean by saying that it wasn't gradual? Maybe the actual writing wasn't gradual—a year and a half is rather rapid, I guess, at least when it's compared with, say, the age of the earth. But getting synchronized into one another's thinking patterns and language preferences—that was gradual, or at least seemed so. A slow motion, underwater experience of inhabiting someone else's mind and style.

Lil: Funny isn't it—that through all this time of writing, that through all the pages and pages of rough drafts, deadends, master copies, and letters to Bob—journal entry after journal entry reads: Vara—protocols; Melinda—chapter on journals; save Sat. for time if needed (that meant we will work on Sat.); think about intro.; make notes on Teacher Talk; talk to Lee about how chapter three is going with her class. Not one mention about how we got the idea in the first place.

Several years ago—really about three—Vara and I were in a class taught by Gordon Pradl, a required practicum on teaching expository writing at New York University. One of Gordon's assignments was to do a profile of someone as a writer, a student preferably, or ourselves. This seemed a strange and difficult task; certainly it was something I had never thought of doing before, though I soon learned that "the writing process" is something teachers of writing spend a lot of time talking about, and the assignment really wasn't so uncommon at all. I chose to write about myself because I had put off the assignment so long that I didn't have time to find a willing student subject. Moreover, I had put off the assignment so long that even after a week's respite because of the overwhelming number of procrastinators in the class, I still had only about 36 hours left. True to form, those 36 hours quickly became 26, and I had no choice but to begin writing the story of myself as a writer.

Lil: Let's see—three years ago when Vara and Melinda were in Gordon's class, I was teaching writing at the University of North Carolina—Wilmington. If someone had told me I would be living in New York one year later, much less writing a book, I would have thought they were crazy. A Southern gal to my bones, I thought only the brave or Hollywood actors would dare walk the streets of Manhattan. On every corner, easily identifiable, were mad rapists

> or mass murderers. I still ask myself how I got to New York
> (that's not in my journal either), but I did and I'm here and
> it isn't anything like I thought it would be.

What I learned from my own writing process paper was that I
had a whole lot to say about my own writing behavior. Odd how whenever I had performed well, either in my student days or writing for a
living, it was always under circumstances of composing a paper an
hour before it was due, spending all night to write a seminar paper to
turn it in at 8:45 the next morning before the secretaries arrived (so it
would look like it had been placed in the professor's mailbox the night
before), meeting a deadline by hopping a cab in midtown Manhattan
with not even minutes to spare, and proofreading an article while
standing in line at the post office hoping to meet the 5 p.m. Express
Mail deadline that would prove I mailed the review on the day it was
due. Strange how whenever my writing has been criticized negatively,
not constructively (doesn't the word *criticism* always imply something
negative?), it was always when I deviated from my own procrastina-
tive routine, ignoring my particular writing process, if you will. Always when I would try to follow the "rules of good writing"—
formulate your thesis statement carefully, construct a detailed outline, summarize your research on note cards, above all PLAN—I
couldn't write well. I would be stricken with that horrible feeling of
saying the same thing over and over again, of feeling and sounding
more and more vapid. There was, I suspected, something terribly
wrong with me. And I might feel even worse when someone worthy of
being called a critic would say on a piece written in my usual manner:
"Careful, well-thought-out, shows a lot of work." Hah!

> **Vara:** But, aside from the writing profile assignment,
> which was a real eyeopener for everyone in the class—re-
> member finding out that every single person—all thirty
> five or so*—was guilty of procrastination? What a revela-
> tion—we didn't have to feel guilty any more—it was part of
> the writing process, legitimate, even somehow appropriate
> and essential to put off writing. Gordon's class though—to
> finish the thought—was our starting point for the book be-
> cause it was our introduction to the teaching of writing as a
> systematic, philosophical act. But I think there were proba-
> bly other starting points. I mean, one brings one's entire life
> experience to bear on each piece of writing, however insig-
> nificant. And this was not a small, insignificant piece of
> writing.
>
> **Bob:** *Including Gordon.

So what I learned from doing an analysis of my own writing process was that I had to determine what *worked* for me, and forget what I was *supposed* to do. It occurred to me then that other people might be experiencing feelings similar to mine. Wouldn't it be useful for *any* writer to do an analysis of his or her writing process. I began to experiment with this idea in the writing classes I was teaching. (Some of those students are represented in this book.) The point of the exercise is to determine, as I did, the strategies that work, the behaviors that don't. Those of us who are procrastinators found out that we had to plan around our procrastination. Easy to say that if I have an article due Wednesday at noon and have to teach Tuesday night, I would finish it Tuesday morning. Somehow, I can always manage to fall asleep or have a pressing errand at the bank. What that means is that to meet any deadline, I must plan to leave free the time immediately before the due date. Those of us who compose only at a typewriter know that we have to be near a typewriter when some writing is to be done. (You can't decide to leave town for a few days or write in the library and above all, don't ever let your typewriter break.)

> **Vara:** But now you've got me thinking about my own writing process paper by contrast with yours. I did turn my paper in right on schedule—I only procrastinated about typing it up until the night before it was due. I had written about a third of it out longhand (my usual strategy, as I realized when I was analyzing my writing habits for the project) and then composed the rest of the thing right in the typewriter, using erasable bond paper and using up two typewriter erasers. It's bad for typewriters, I know, but it's the only way that I can do it—an ingrained habit. When it comes to procrastination, I usually try to meet the deadline head on and I try not to ask for extensions from anybody— extensions release the tension of anxiety and anxiety is also a crucial feature of my composing process—I have to get worked up into a foaming terror before I can really crank anything out. Self-destructive? Neurotic? Maybe so. But at least, it works. Usually. Once, I was under too much pressure, and my brain sort of went "sproing" at two in the morning. I couldn't finish the thing. I had to start again several days later after the burnout effect had worn off.
>
> **Lil:** I'm not a procrastinator like Melinda, but I'm not a "formulate your thesis statement" type person either. I'm organized, but I never outline. I'm just a sit-down-and-get-it-done-so-that-I-don't-have-think-about-it-anymore type writer. I write, try my ideas out on whoever will listen, write

some more, try it out again, write. I can't wait until the last minute because I need plenty of time to bother a bunch of folks about what I am writing. I thrive on feedback. I'm never satisfied with what is there because my ideas grow and change. That is why I need a deadline. I quit when it is due. I just go with what I have.

Meanwhile, about the time I was exploring the idea of writing being a process, I was becoming increasingly dissatisfied with composition textbooks available. Almost everything I read flatly contradicted what I knew about the way writers write. And what seemed most offensive were all those books that presented beautiful pieces of finished prose to examine as models—the college reader. I say offensive because they never show how they were produced; they never show the writing in process.

Lil: I always hated every composition textbook I taught from. They made writing look as if it were easy—just slot your ideas into a form. But my ideas were always round and amorphous whereas those forms were square and rigid. I always wrote my outline last, once the paper was finished. I could never follow one. I often changed my mind about what I was saying once I began to see what I had to say. I was never neat and tidy. I always began, backed up, changed my mind, and began again.

Vara: Well, when it comes to composition texts, we were all totally disgruntled, yes? (I mean, there are a few exceptions, but the majority are a pretty standardized lot). The typical composition text covers the traditional dogmas of the teaching of writing with all the innovative flair and brilliance of a fast-food restaurant menu. And of course, you're right, the majority of texts are in direct and obstinate opposition to the way writers actually write. Wasn't it a brainstorm to realize as we were putting our students through the rigors of multiple drafts, that those lovely essays by E. B. White and Joan Didion were so terribly intimidating to the inexperienced writer precisely because they were absolutely perfect and polished—there *were* no false starts and new beginnings. And then, we realized that the best mix of all would be juxtaposing student and professional work because, that way, some of the mystique of the "real" writer would be undermined and the student writer could begin to see that the art of writing wasn't the result of inspiration but of grueling (yet rewarding) blood, sweat, and tears.

During my first year of teaching composition, Paula Johnson, director of the writing program at NYU, mentioned several times how useful it would be to have a collection of essays written by students in our own program. What an ingenious idea! Students could create their own textbook for their own writing program, but we realized that most useful of all would be to present student writing in multiple drafts.

> **Lil:** Do you remember the MEMO? One weekend after I got to NYU, I sat down and wrote up what I believed would be the minimum commitment for writing a book—a real torture routine. Days and days, weeks and weeks, years and years of writing and meeting and working collaboratively. Little did I know that the time table was less than adequate. What I managed to do, however, was scare off those who really didn't want to write a book but only thought they did. Vara and Melinda said they were willing to sign on the project. And they did. And we did. And the days grew into weeks, the weeks into years.

I can't say exactly when this idea for a book surfaced among our community of writing teachers, but it was sometime after my revelatory experience in Gordon Pradl's class in the fall of 1979. We let all these ideas bounce around for a while until the winter of 1980–81. (Why start on something before you have a deadline?) But what Vara and I did do during all that time was collect samples of student and professional work. Meanwhile, we were part of writing groups both inside classrooms and outside of them, formal meetings and informal conversations over a cup of coffee or a bottle of beer.

One day we sat down and decided we really should put our heads together and make use of what we had learned and discovered. By this time Lil had joined the program as director of the Writing Center (and assistant director of the program itself), and she was eager to see a process-oriented textbook materialize. (And she would not allow us to procrastinate further.)

> **Vara:** This bit about how "Lil had joined the program as director of the Writing Center" reminded me of the first time I ever met her. It was when she came to NYU for her interview and, as it happened, I was the only teacher around that afternoon. We talked for nearly an hour, mostly about what it's like surviving in New York City and what it's like teaching at NYU. Lil wanted to know the lowdown so she could compare the possibility of living in the big city with the known quantity of living in Wilmington. I thought she was wonderful and hoped like mad that she'd be offered the

job. Of course, she was and she accepted it. Even in the first few months of the Writing Center's existence, of Lil's presence at NYU, neither Melinda nor I had the slightest idea that soon we would all three be working on this project together.

For the three of us, once we started working together, our most important initial idea for such a book was to dispel all the misconceptions of the revising process. My journal notes for early March stress that we channel all the work in terms of professional and student writing. We decided on a tentative organizing principle: writers revising in different ways. Our first table of contents included about 16 categories. (Being a compulsive journal keeper myself, I meticulously kept one especially for "the book.")

Vara: I escaped getting ground up in the gears of the rules of good writing. I think mostly I ignored them, seeing them as superfluous. When I was taught to diagram sentences, I took it as a game, sort of like crossword puzzles and with just about the same amount of direct transference to my writing. When it came to writing a "persuasive" essay in my undergraduate composition class, I obediently learned the "theory" and then did not even attempt to apply it to my actual writing. I did use to summarize my research on notecards, or rather, I used to take prolific, nay, obsessive, verbatim notes on my reading, but I have since gotten out of the habit (laziness) and I regret it.

Within a short period of time we had collected a vast amount of student work from the classes we had been teaching. We investigated professional writing as well. Our preliminary list of published writers included Henry James, F. Scott Fitzgerald, Franz Kafka, Charles Dickens, Flannery O'Connor, Joan Didion, Ernest Hemingway, Virginia Woolf—enough for several books. Finding the student work was easy. Deciding which of it to use wasn't. Just as we all had our own ways of writing, we also had our own ways of reading. What Vara liked, I didn't. What one of us considered good revision, the other didn't. (What is "good" revision anyway?) We agreed to read and reread and revise our notions of good writing.

Vara: The whole project has been a process of negotiation from beginning to end. Seemingly irrelevant disputes over wording have as often as not been catalysts for clarifying our most fundamental concepts, even as selecting the student papers to use helped us to decide what it was that we were really trying to say about writing.

Lil: Learning *how* to read a text is no easy matter. I keep asking myself, "What kind of reader is this text inviting me to be?" Rarely does anyone want a text to be read by a TEACHER whose only function is to find fault with the writing. When I write I want my reader to become engaged with the ideas I'm presenting. I want my reader to understand my intentions. I want my reader to explore the meaning I've created. If my thoughts are not conveyed, I rewrite trying to bring closer together my intentions and the effects my words have on the reader. I wish often I could do it right the first time. I never do.

Finding multiple-draft examples of professional writers was far from easy. Not quite like looking for a four-leaf clover (substitute any cliché you like here), but it seemed that way at times. No one has put together an easily accessible (one that I could find anyway) study focusing on the composing processes of professional writers. I had to investigate each author any of us thought had possibilities. Of course, we were convinced that all writers revise, but what we needed was the evidence—most of which simply did not seem to exist.

I remembered Henry James's notebooks from a paper I did for part of my graduate work, but the book was checked out of the library. (A feeble excuse, I know, but. . . .) There didn't seem to be a copy of the facsimile edition of *The Waste Land* anywhere in New York. I thought this book would show how Ezra Pound served as a writing group of one for T.S. Eliot. (Later, it didn't matter because only one/two of us even understood *The Waste Land* anyway.) I knew that somewhere there was a letter written by Fitzgerald to Hemingway telling his friend to "cut the nonsense" in the first part of *The Sun Also Rises.* But how could I find it? There didn't seem to be a set of letters between Fitzgerald and Hemingway. Finally, I ran across a copy of *The Correspondence of F. Scott Fitzgerald,* and I read letter after letter until I found a clue to what I wanted. I was lucky that time.

At other times I read through voluminous amounts of stuff without finding anything worthwhile. For instance, in all of Max Perkins's letters I didn't find a single one that had a direct correspondence to changes in one of his author's works. (I even read the new biography of him to see if someone else had run across what I wanted.) Yet I did find some useful quotes on the role of editors (what we have come to call, in our book, "experienced readers"). It wouldn't be an exaggeration to say that I spent weeks in several libraries—and research is like writing, you have to go through a lot of false starts, dead-ends, aborted leads before you discover something you can use, and you find out what you want or what you think by undergoing this process of trial and error. And you collect a lot more material than you can ever use.

> **Lil:** While Melinda cloistered herself in New York libraries, I was trying to drum up interest in our book with various publishers. Several were interested in the idea, but they had a fixed agenda about what would sell. In other words, they wanted us to write about things we didn't believe in (like every paragraph having a topic sentence). I knew I could never write a book about writing if I had to write the book in a different way from the way I actually write myself or in a different way from what I knew about how anyone else actually writes. It seemed crazy to perpetuate the same old myth about good writing.

Finally, after gathering all this evidence of the writing process—both student and professional—we sent it off to Bob Boynton, organized by category under the tentative contents page we had devised. Then we waited. Meanwhile, we hadn't done any writing. What we mailed Bob weighed at least as much as a whole ham, excluding excess fat. The manuscript, if you could call it that, was entitled *Writers Revising*. As we said to Bob, "We want to make public, for the first time for student writers, how writers go about writing."

> **Vara:** In retrospect, it seems to me that Bob's agreeing to look at the manuscript was the most exciting moment of the entire year and a half. We were still in the innocent stages of our enthusiasm, long before the frustrations and drudgery of the real work had taken the edge off our delight, and it was an incredible rush to realize that this experimental and unconventional effort of ours actually had half a chance of seeing print.

Bob's response was something on the order of "you have some terrific material here but what in the world are you going to do with it?" I suppose that initially we thought we could simply present examples of revision in process without any explanation (suspiciously like the model readers: what we had were model revisions. Hmmm.). At the same time my journal for the book includes piles of notes on what kinds of stuff still needed to be collected, rather than what needed to be done with what we had already accumulated.

Bob: A few comments from my letter to you after receiving the bundle—and after being reminded by phone that I was sitting on it longer than promised—will show the kinds of things that concerned me initially, and did or did not concern you eventually:

"You say that it's a book for both students & teachers, and that's good, but I think, if it's going to be used (sold) as a student text, that students have to be the primary audience. Your introduction is addressed to them (and to teachers-as-writers, which is a good way to think of teachers all through the book), but I think you need to keep asking yourselves how much of a given strategy or example most students can, or will, take in at a given time and how each one can be tied into something they're doing or are asked to do. If the book is a writer as well as a reader, it has to be a writer for the students using it. You say that it's "not a *how to* book but a *knowing about* book," but, in a real sense, it's both, with the *how to* part wedded to the *knowing about* part as students (I assume) do their daily stints of writing, not in imitation of what they see other writers having done but certainly informed by what they see. . . .

"Do you intend to include commentary on the various examples included, where you feel the revision was particularly effective, or not effective? Will you ask the students to do the same thing? I'm sure that this kind of thing goes on in class. Is there any way you can ensure (or try to) that it goes on in classes you aren't connected with? In other words, do you expect the readers of the book to interact with the examples as well as be enlightened by them? (I'd like to tell Bill Atwill why I think the first para. of his first draft is better than the revisions.) In a few cases, I'm not sure that the revisions have done much to improve things and that they're worth the reworking. Is that a legitimate issue to raise?

"You've undoubtedly used the questionnaire, so you know how well it works. Do people actually respond to all the questions or simply use them for suggestions about what to consider? (I found the suggestion at the end to "use the rest of your time writing down any of your thoughts . . ." delightful; it would take me all afternoon and all of prime time to write my answers "out in full," as you put it. You intend to shorten it (good) and add to it: I'll give you a question for nothing: "How do you start dealing with an 'assigned paper'? How do you think you *should* go about it? Were you ever *taught* how to do it? If you don't do it that way, why not?" Why not start off with the questionnaire, in its shortened form? Get them doing something, not just reading what somebody else does."

Like Brian Santo, when the deadlines wouldn't go away, we had to become writers. We discovered lots of writing that needed to be done. We needed to find a way to show readers how to use the book that had yet to be written. We needed exercises (what a dreadful sounding word). We needed notes to introduce each unit (that wonderful term, of course, used primarily in textbooks). Under our original plan we had divided chapters into what we perceived as being individual concepts, or units.

Lil: Remember all the revising we had to do—how we wrote all morning long to produce five typed pages; how we gave them to Cy to read over lunch and he found problems on every page; how we would spend all afternoon trying to figure out exactly what we meant? Remember how we would think we had a chapter just perfect—how we would send it out for teachers to try out in their classes; how when we got their responses we knew exactly what we did wrong; how we would try again to figure out exactly what we meant? Remember Bob's comments and all the revisions he made us make (like adding four more chapters)? Our first drafts were never like our final ones.

Bob: The editor's lot is a happy one. It's easier (and more useful) raising questions and making suggestions than it is going back to the drawing board to deal with them. Writing teachers would find their lot easier (and more useful) if they stopped seeing themselves as surgeons or exorcists and stopped treating every piece of writing as a finished product or a plot to bring on premature aging. Once the teacher renounces the fixer's role and adopts the nurturer's one, the whole learning situation changes. (That said, I have to add that I hope Lil's comment about "all the revisions he made us make" is playfully put. "Suggested," not "made." Especially since some of my suggestions you wisely ignored, or wished you had.)

We each took a chapter to "rough out"—our lingo, at the time, for writing a draft. Upon reconvening, we discovered, as we should have known, that all three of us sounded radically different. Meanwhile, we were (or seemed to be) addressing each other rather than our readers. Who were our readers?

What we discovered is that we had to discover what we wanted to say as we were writing. We thought we knew, but we didn't. We thought it would be easy; it wasn't. (And talk about not practicing what you preach.)

> **Vara:** This just goes to prove that writing really is recursive, but I have no intention of trying to define "recursive." The tussle we had over that word! Did we really spend almost two hours (the distortion of memory, no doubt) trying to define it to our own satisfaction so that we could define it for student readers? In the end, it was easier to delete it than to define it. A minor revision necessitated by the implied audience. But perfectly illustrative of the revision process—the writing-and-revising process I should say. So often, one sweats and stews and suffers trying to save some choice tidbit, lovely word or sentence, some image or tangential digression—only to realize, after a vast "waste" of time, that it is hopelessly irrelevant or incompatible. The sacrifice then is a relief, not a tragedy—almost painless. But I put "waste" in quotations because I don't think anything is wasted in the process of writing—the mind is always working out problems, some of which haven't even materialized yet, and it's only through the terrible wrestling that the language can be shaped and the meaning elicited from the cloud of inspiration.

We felt, at the time, that one of our biggest problems was tone. (Translation: Who were our readers?) But in trying to adjust the tone, we were still discovering what we wanted to say. In other words, we were rewriting to meet the needs of our intended readers, and in that process, we were finding out and changing what we were seeing—we were revising while we were writing. What? (Should we be surprised?) In the process of writing this book, we discovered our major point: revising is no different from writing; they are, indeed, the same process. Hence, we changed the title of our opus to *Writers Writing* from *Writers Revising*.

> **Vara:** So much has to be left out and starting points are so arbitrary.
>
> **Bob:** And so are ending points. I like the comment quoted earlier that a piece of writing is never finished, just abandoned. Like this chapter.

Suggestions for Teachers

(Not for Teachers Only)

The material and ideas for this book came from our own experiences as teachers and researchers, writers and readers. We would like to share with you how we envision the book's use and why we wrote it the way we did.

First the why (the theory):

When you teach writing, you're teaching a complex activity involving many repeated choices about what to say and where and how to say it. Most textbooks on the market today, although they may use words such as "process," "invention," and "discovery" (words which denote this complex activity), in fact, implicitly deny the real meanings of these words in their teaching recommendations. The reason, perhaps, that these books teach "the usual hogwash" (rhetorical modes, paragraph patterns, thesis statements, and topic sentences), despite the use of seemingly modern terminology, is that the theory which underlies these books is based on a classical model of rhetoric. The components of composition within the classical framework come from an analysis of the product, a description of what characterizes a finished piece of discourse. Teachers' concerns, then, are not with how a writer comes to know a subject through making choices in the act of writing, but with the presentation of ideas in certain genres (or with what writing should look like). There's no discovery of ideas; ideas are something the writer starts out with, perhaps in an outline, and then slots into prefabricated forms—for example, a compare/contrast model. The major preoccupation is with form itself and correctness of grammar and mechanics.

Even in the best textbooks using this model, writing is reduced to the completion of various "stages" of development: first the writer prewrites (finds an idea), then writes, and finally revises (revision being controlled by a checklist with questions like "Is your introduction interesting?" or "Does each paragraph have one idea?"). Although on the surface this may look to teachers like writing-as-discovery, it really isn't. Writers don't first "discover" what they want to say (before beginning to write), then write their ideas, and finally revise them.

These activities are not discrete and consecutive. Writing and discovery, forming and thinking, happen all at once. Writing-and-revising is one act, the process of making meaning.

What, then, is the theory which underlies this book? Writing is not the display of what a writer has already learned; rather, it is the verbal manifestation of the writer's capacity to learn by making connections in diverse experience. Writing is a way of knowing, of learning more and more about a subject. Knowing is not something a writer starts out with, and it's not a static body of information that a person acquires. Knowing is an activity and writing is one representation of this activity. Writing is the discovering and shaping of thought in language; the writer's use of language represents the connections she has made, the active relating of one bit of information to another.

A teacher does not really "teach" writing at all. One could simply tell students the choices that they must make, but doing so would be only to explain something abstractly, not to show what the activity of choosing is really like. Imagine teaching someone how to ride a bicycle by explaining that he must point the front wheel in the same direction as the weight of his body. Although the explanation is descriptively adequate, it certainly doesn't aid the learner to stay up on the bike. Just as one learns to ride a bicycle by riding it, one learns to write by practicing writing. It's the teacher's responsibility to create a classroom environment where this learning can take place, a context where student writers can experiment, trying out a line of reasoning wherever it may take them, saying something one way and then saying it another. The concern, then, is not for packaging information but for fluency, not for the mastery of certain predefined constraints, but for emerging form. In this context, the writer's ideas, her intentions to say and do certain things, are what matters. The teacher provides a place where the writer can feel free to take risks, to experiment with different ways of saying things. This context is a writing workshop.

Now to the teaching (the practice):

A writing workshop is a place where students write, share their writing with readers, and rewrite to meet the needs of those readers. By writing, reading what they have written, and hearing the response of readers, students see that writing is genuine communication. They are no longer giving back information to a teacher who already knows the answers, but are finding and conveying their own meanings to readers who are genuinely interested in what they have to say. If their ideas do not come across to the audience, the writers must reformulate them, trying again to say what they mean. If they jump too quickly from one assertion to the next or if the reader becomes confused, unable to see the relationships among assertions, the writer must go back, rewrite, attempt to show the connections more precisely.

Students learn to write by becoming more and more conscious of the choices they make and the effect those choices have on readers. This awareness comes when they sense that the reader depends on those choices in order to understand what the writers are saying. Thus, it's important in a writing workshop to fill the classroom with student readers, people who engage in dialogue with the writer about the writer's text, showing through the questions that they ask the need for more connection-making, more writing. The aim of this dialogue is for writers to internalize the questions that readers have, thereby enabling the writer to improve through an increased capacity to make choices. Perhaps the best form for this dialogue is a writing group of no more than five students. A transcript of a writing group discussion is provided in Chapter 7.

Responding as readers is not difficult once students learn that their responsibility in a writing group is not to correct or "fix" a piece of writing. Their responsibility is to give the writer their perceptions of what is being said and their reactions to it. The writer solely is responsible for the ideas; she knows best what she wants to say and what effect she's trying to create. The readers know best the actual effect the writer's choices have on them. Sharing this information is the point of a writing group. And through negotiation, by bringing closer and closer together the writer's sense of what she wants to say and the readers' perceptions of actual effects, the writer learns to communicate. A model for the responding process can be found in Chapters 6, 7, and 8.

In order to help writers discover what they want to say, this book offers strategies that other writers have used to record their perceptions and make meaning of them through writing. Chapter 4 focuses on how professional and student writers keep journals, not only of how different events shape their lives but also of how they have gone about composing. Whether, like Hawthorne, they use their notebooks to shape images which may eventually, even years later, find their way into their writing, or, like James, they use their journals to talk with themselves about the shape of a story, students will see that ideas evolve from the chaos of their everyday experiences, that their intention to say something comes from the way they begin to perceive their lives as meaningful. A crucial feature of a writing workshop is, therefore, that students get into the habit of keeping journals. Seldom does writing spring fully edited from the pen. Instead, days, even years, of writing and thinking, forming and experimenting, looking and looking again, go into the making of meaning

Even when writers think they have "nothing to say," Chapter 5 will offer them ways of tapping their forming powers through writing.

Often, inexperienced writers need strategies for getting started and need to be encouraged not to move to closure too quickly. The method called free-writing, which this chapter describes, will demonstrate how writers have freed themselves of the many blocks which stop their choice-making and, by writing nonstop, have generated new ideas and new directions their writing could take. The chapter also offers ways to "force" oneself to revise. By changing perspective (the strategy demonstrated late in the chapter), writers put off closure by making new connections and seeing different directions that their writing can take.

All the writing in this book will become meaningful only in workshops where the students' own writing and their attitudes about it are the central concern of the course. In order for students to start seeing themselves as writers, this book begins with a questionnaire, an inventory of what students think about writing and themselves as writers. Often, students have been schooled into believing many myths about good writers. They think that good writers never revise. In fact, many think revision is a punishment for not getting it right the first time. If students revise at all, it's simply to change a word here and there. Chapter 2 gives examples of writers writing about their composing processes, showing students that experienced writers also have anxieties and frustrations, false starts and idiosyncracies. Then in Chapter 3 students will see the various drafts the writer worked from. The evolving meanings and their changes are there for students to inspect and to learn from. Above all, it's important to establish and reinforce a sense of community among the writers in your classroom and between them and the writers in this book.

Here are some ideas for adapting the material in this book to your workshop:

This book is meant as a resource to enrich the material of your workshop classroom. Because your students' own writing is the central concern of the course, this book is not meant to be a substitute for student discussion about their own writing; rather it provides a means of showing what choices other writers made in order to create new meaning and gives a model of the activities that writers engage in. We suggest that the course begin and end with the questionnaire provided in Chapter 1. This inventory asks writers to survey their attitudes and feelings about writing and themselves as writers, and to compare their responses to those of other writers. At the beginning of the course, students often have little to say about their writing. Often, their experiences with writing are limited, their attitudes restricted. If the course does what it should, your students, by the end of the semester, will see that they have grown more aware of their writing process and more adept at seeing their writing in new ways.

We have given you Writing-and-Revising assignments, and you should select those which will match the interests and needs of your students. We encourage you to have them bring in writing from other courses, from work-related situations, whatever. The Interactions related to the essays in each chapter also give students the opportunity to write and to interact with their peers in order to learn. We do suggest that you assign only one essay to read in all its drafts at one time and that you select or even design your own interactions appropriate to your own teaching concerns. In other words, don't overload students by assigning a chapter in its entirety, but choose appropriate examples as they are needed.

You may want to begin with the questionnaire and work your way through the book one paper at a time. Another, and perhaps better way to use the book would be to assign students to read one paper from the book in all its drafts as the concepts it demonstrates seem applicable to the needs of the class. Suppose, for example, that during the answering of the questionnaire you determine that many of your students have trouble getting started writing. For the next class period you might have them read Brian Santo's writing process paper so they see that a good student writer has the same problem. After discussing that essay you might have them look at the free-writing strategy explained in Chapter 5 for a way of getting ideas on paper or Chapter 4 where Virginia Woolf says that, although she, too, often has "nothing to say," by writing, she discovers things that matter to her.

Some helpful hints:

1. Remember that students will respond to their classmates just as teachers respond to them. Your comments on student writing, oral and written, should serve as a model for your students. If you take their meanings seriously and respond as a supportive reader to the ideas in their papers, they'll respond as supportive readers to other members of the class.

2. Most students have had little experience revising their work. They're only accustomed to changing a word here and there. Exhortations to revise will fall on deaf ears. Students must be encouraged to trust in the power of re-envisioning their work and be supported in their efforts to do so.

3. Essays from the text should be used to look inductively at the strategies of other writers. Once students see how a writer has changed a draft, they should try the strategy out on their own writing. There is no substitute for the students' own writing.

4. Students should write for their own purposes and for real readers who are interested in what they have to say. They should be encouraged to research their ideas to add depth and richness to

their experiences and to write for readers who demand accuracy and precision. Most students will, of course, need guidance in using the library—in particular, the research assignments in this book require the use of primary sources. Your students' ideas should be taken as seriously as those of any published writer.

Just as teachers ask students to seek readers' responses to help determine the effect their writing creates, so we asked other teachers and students to use a draft of this book in their own writing workshop classes in order to help us re-envision the text and to see if our ideas were transferable to their contexts. However, they did not have all the chapters now included here or the finished version of the ones they did receive. It was with their help that this book evolved into the text you now hold. Because we learned from their experiences, we thought you too would like to learn how a few of them—Cindy Onore, Lee Leeson, Bob Leonard, and Bill Burns—have used some of the material in the book.

Cynthia Onore

What all unpracticed writers seem to share is their inability to revise despite whether the desire to do so is self-initiated or imposed by instructors. No matter how often I have directed my students to rework their papers, what I tend to get from them is a draft with a word change here, a sentence deleted there, or oftentimes, a new conclusion on an otherwise intact discourse. This pattern was disrupted, though, when my students became familiar with the revision strategies in *Writers Writing* and tried them out. What this text seems to offer is a way for newcomers to revision to be presented dramatically with their own tacit powers to resee their texts. By this I simply mean to imply that our student writers have, without conscious awareness of them, the necessary tools for seeing again their discourses, but that these resources are simply not engaged by the instruction from a teacher to "Revise!" By taking seriously the notion that to revise is to resee, the techniques offered here create a context in which a writer can't help but intuitively engage in this reseeing process.

One activity that worked particularly well happened early in the semester. After the class had studied several essays in Chapter 5, I assigned them to reread the entire chapter, paying particular attention to the way writers changed perspective. I followed this assignment up by asking during individual conference time for each student to choose one piece of work from his or her portfolio and to change perspective and revise it. This perspective change could involve either a shift in point of view or a decision to begin the text in a new place. Since no two students were working on the same assignment, this experiment was performed on writing in a variety of rhetorical contexts.

Our course procedures allowed each student time to begin his or her "forced revision" during our conference time, and as a result, I could observe exactly what took place. Within ten or fifteen minutes of my direction to "Change perspective!" each writer had begun anew, consequently re-seeing both meaning and intention. During the following class session, each writer read to the writing group the original draft of the text and the new draft. We all concurred that the transformations in the texts were dramatic and impressive. Not only did the respondents concur, but the writer, too, could grasp the range of choices which had become available by way of this exercise. Each change in perspective or beginning fostered other changes and like the "domino effect," the process was automatic.

Lee Ann Leeson

There are twenty students in this Writing Workshop I class—most of them eighteen year old freshmen from the New York City area educated in public schools. There are a few older transfer students. For six students English is a second language, and for three, this is their first year in the United States.

Although this is an "average" class, the writing profile assignment indicates that as writers these students are far from homogeneous. Last year, my first at NYU, I had made the all too common mistake of basing most inferences about my student writers on the papers they produced. When the papers were not skillfully written, I often assumed such things as: A. the student had little experience as a writer, B. the student probably didn't like to write, C. the student had spent little time on the assignment. While all of these things were true some of the time for some writers, writing profiles and the discussion they generated indicated a much more complex picture. We went over the writing questionnaire in our first class and wrote out answers for our second. During this second class hour, students interviewed each other in pairs and used this information to prepare writing profiles of their partners. These profiles ran about one typed page long, and each student brought in twenty copies of his or her paper to distribute in our next class session. Each profile was read aloud to the whole group and we responded, not criticizing the writing, but asking questions or commenting on various points the profile made about the writer and writing. This got a bit tedious with a group of twenty, and, perhaps, we should have read some papers in smaller groups and only a few as a whole class. I wanted, though, to introduce all of these students to the idea that in our workshop they were producing writing to be read by me and by other students, and that responding to writing doesn't just mean pointing our errors or criticizing but responding to what the writer says. I wanted them to begin to think of themselves as writers, to begin to be introspective about their own writing experience and process, and to see how they were alike or different from other writers.

The next step was to ask students to write writing profiles of themselves. For the personal writing profile, a deeper analysis was encouraged, and, as we would with all other assignments in the semester, we worked to write several drafts, several different versions of this paper. First drafts, which students shared in small groups, tended to be superficial. In response to this draft and to a second draft that I commented on in writing, we tried to use questions to encourage writers to go deeper. What overall impression of you as a writer emerges from this paper? Why? What could you do either to change this impression or to develop it further? If your first step is, say, deciding what to write about, how do you decide? How did you get started writing this assignment?

The results were informative. We discovered that most students in the class made a definite distinction between writing they had to do for a grade—essays and reports— and writing that was either ungraded or that they did for themselves—journals, letters, poems. Most of them liked the latter sort of writing and felt that the former was mainly a matter of finding out what the teacher wanted and then trying, somehow, to produce it. I discovered that the dullest kind of five paragraph essay was often the result of years of practice and a source of considerable pride for many students. I resolved not to make last year's mistake of simply rejecting this as the work of an unskilled writer, but to build on the student's confidence and encourage experimentation with different forms.

While some students gained and conveyed new insights in each successive draft of their profiles, other papers stayed pretty much the same through three rewrites. Many students explained that, beyond correcting spelling and recopying in neat handwriting, they had never revised a paper before and had no idea of what I meant by revision. While in my past teaching I had routinely exhorted students to revise, the examples in Chap. 3 gave me a way of showing how and why this might be done. In the first place, these pieces illustrate that revision is not a punishment for "bad" writing. These are "good" student papers to begin with. Secondly, students can see that extensive revision does not simply state the same meaning in a better way but, in fact, can create new meaning. And thirdly, the examples in Chap. 3 demonstrate that there are no easy formulas for writing. Writers have to make their own choices.

I asked them to write analyses of their own revision, frankly insisting that they make changes substantive enough to be analyzed. I stressed revision as a key strategy not because it necessarily makes student writing better (in fact, sometimes papers get worse) but because making changes forces writers to make choices, and learning to control these choices to convey meaning and affect readers is in many ways what we mean by learning to write.

We referred to *Writers Writing* again toward the end of the semester to explore the role of research in writing. Rather than beginning with the artificial formulas in a "how to write research papers" guide, we again questioned writer choices. For example, what does research material add to Timothy Tseng's narrative? Why did he footnote this material? If he published this as a short story in a magazine would he still need footnotes? Why not? How would Dianne Ray have gone about locating her material in our library? What's the purpose of her bibliography? Why didn't Patrick McGrath have to document his sources? If he needed documentation to publish his work in a scholarly music journal, how could he go about it? This approach again, I think, looks at the process of writing and not at just a final product, in this case called the research paper.

Writers Writing raises questions and provides opportunities for asking many others. Answers may vary and this is uncomfortable for many students. This text will work best in classrooms where the questions themselves are valued as a way of probing choices writers make and the effect these choices have on readers.

Robert Leonard

High school writers have been trained to believe in two great myths. The first is that essays and compositions spring full blown from the pen of a writer, much like Athene from the forehead of Zeus. Students think they emerge in finished form, with only technical errors to correct—and those are left to the red pen of the teacher/evaluator, not the writer. The second myth is that essays and compositions, once spawned, are not written in pen and ink, but are graven in stone. What is written is written, and any thought of revision is anathema.

I found these myths to be alive, well, and flourishing in my Advanced Methods of Composition course in September of 1981. I had designed the course to train high school juniors and seniors to become peer tutors in our new Writing Center. My students were bright and eager, and had experienced success in their school writing. Unfortunately, their experience in writing had made them believers in the Two Great Myths. When I started preaching the gospel of process writing they were polite and attentive, but their writing showed that in their heart of hearts, they still clung to the old pattern of "one in pencil, one in ink."

During the first week of class we worked on having each tutor discover his or her own idiosyncratic writing process; to break out of the shell of writing to fill in the blanks of an outline. I was struggling against the accumulated years of prior training by teachers who were product oriented. The free-writing exercises went all right, but my fledgling tutors still composed final drafts on their first attempt. When I mentioned this problem to Lil Brannon, she suggested that I try *Writers Writing*, which was still in manuscript form. There was immediate recognition and delight as my students began to read Brian Santo's "The Reason God Made Hands." The honest confession of procrastinating before writing, the asides, the (√)'s, all served to teach some valuable lessons: that writers put off writing, that writers work in peculiar places, and that writing is finally done under the sword of the deadline. Brian's relaxed style, his verbal puns, his diagrams and folksy style showed, better than a thousand lectures, that writing could be serious without being dull. It also gave the students the incentive to write some really honest and introspective analyses of themselves as writers. The writing profiles which followed were far more honest and far less sonorous and pedantic.

We compared writing profiles (me, too!) and saw that outlines and fill-in-the-blank essays were really stifling a much more fluid procedure. One boy confessed that he fought writer's block by lying on the floor to help him think. Most of the students admitted that outlines were usually done after, not before compositions were written. Brian's essay helped to establish a feeling of community and put the first big fissure in Myth #1.

Kathryn Lance's "How I Write" assaulted Myth #2. When my tutors read that she revised upwards of sixteen times, they were appalled. Nevertheless, the essay gave my writers the courage to revise from what they had learned was "mud," not a finished product. They saw that professionals were no surer of how they wrote than high school students were. "How I Write" taught that there does not have to be a finished product in mind when a writer sits down to write. The key was to keep writing until the writer felt that it was right. The peer tutors began to believe in the writing process, to loosen up, to take risks in revising their own efforts. The two essays the class read and discussed convinced them that free-writing was the best way of "getting it down," of allowing verbal surprise to enter into what might ordinarily be dull stuff, and of generating a host of approaches that the writer might choose from when further drafting took place.

William Burns

I used portions of *Writers Writing* in my student-centered tutorial section at New York University which comprised a small (about six), heterogenous assortment of college students, from different disciplines, most of whom were, to varying degrees, bright although fundamentally unpracticed writers, with different interests and work loads. Most were there because for one reason or another they had failed the writing proficiency exam given at the end of their freshman year; one elected to be there. Their writing handicaps, however, seemed to have resulted more from inexperience and previous bad training than from any cognitive difficulties. The one characteristic common to them all was that they had a very poor image of themselves as writers. Most would rather have been *anywhere* than in a writing course. The greatest problem that I faced, then, was persuading them that they could become competent writers. If I could do that then I could begin to make them want to become competent writers.

I built a lesson early into the course from Chapter 4 on various ways to use a journal. Since I require in all my classes that students keep journals of some kind, I was pleased to find in the text inspiring examples of how different writers—the inexperienced student as well as the experienced author—have used their journals as a repository of ideas and experience that would be developed later into a more formalized public communication. I also found that this wide range of examples of journal writing encouraged students to take risks, to play with different modes of writing. One would-be songwriter used his journal to record, among other things, lyrics to his songs during his breaks in the day. A young artist used her journal as a sketch pad, recording both visual and verbal impressions of subway riders as she commuted back and forth to school every day. Another student used his journal as a work book for expanding his ideas into first drafts of papers for my course.

Because any new class usually involves some degree of anxiety on the part of at least some of the students, I found the first chapter helpful in easing us all into a discussion of writing that would begin the task of replacing, on the one hand, their fear of writing or feelings of inadequacy with useful strategies, and on the other hand, replacing a multitude of reinforced misconceptions about writing, writers, and how it comes about with new ways of looking at writing as process.

The discussion served to warm the atmosphere, especially when they began to see that they shared similar problems and attitudes; it also helped to set the tone and direction of the class: writers talking about writing. The class ended with a discussion centered around "Assumptions About Good Writers" from the next chapter. It fit right into what we were saying so I included it here. At this point most of them still believed that the *modus operandi* of the experienced writer was to sit at the typewriter and in one attempt bang out a publishable piece of writing which he had carefully composed in his head beforehand. But the seeds of doubt for this and other misconceptions had been sown.

As revisors, my students were all basically word changers. They looked for easy solutions to complex problems. Underneath their attitude seemed to lurk the assumption that once something had been committed to paper, communication had been made. If anything was to be changed it was words here and there. It was not until much later in the course, after much practice revising their own work, that I could see some change taking place. The emphasis most of them had placed on revision as a process of cleaning up—fixing errors and changing words—had begun to shift. Now they were beginning to see that revision meant "re-seeing" and sometimes involved a letting go of something already said to make room for something new and better. Not only were examples or words added or deleted, but whole papers reordered, points of view changed, rhetorical strategies switched, frustrating tension endured, and conclusions held in abeyance as new meaning was discovered and made. They had, in fact, begun to behave like writers.